P9-DGJ-300

SOME
PERSONALITY DETERMINANTS
OF THE EFFECTS OF PARTICIPATION

1959 Award Winner

THE FORD FOUNDATION DOCTORAL DISSERTATION SERIES

*A dissertation submitted in partial
fulfillment of the requirements for
the degree of Doctor of Philosophy
at the University of Michigan*

SOME

PERSONALITY DETERMINANTS

OF THE EFFECTS OF PARTICIPATION

VICTOR H. VROOM

Survey Research Center and
Department of Psychology
University of Michigan

P R E N T I C E - H A L L ,   I N C .

Englewood Cliffs, N. J.

155.2
V984s

First printing ....May, 1960
Second printing ....October, 1961

© — *1960 by* PRENTICE-HALL, INC.
Englewood Cliffs, N. J.

*All rights reserved. No part of this book
may be reproduced in any form, by mimeograph or any other means,
without permission in writing from the publishers.*

L. C. Catalog Card Number: 60-11585

• *Printed in The United States of America*
82201 — C

Foreword

This volume is one of five doctoral dissertations selected for publication in the first annual Doctoral Dissertation Competition sponsored by the Program in Economic Development and Administration of The Ford Foundation. The winning dissertations were completed during the academic year 1958-59 by doctoral candidates in business administration and doctoral candidates in the social sciences and other fields relevant to the study of problems of business.

The dissertation competition is intended to generalize standards of excellence in research on business by graduate students. It should give widespread professional recognition to persons recently awarded doctorates in business whose dissertation research is especially distinguished by its analytical content and strong roots in underlying disciplines. It is also intended to give recognition to a select number of persons outside business schools who in their doctoral dissertations pursued with distinction interests relevant to business.

The dissertations selected include, in addition to Dr. Vroom's monograph:

Computer Models of the Shoe, Leather, Hide Sequence
Kalman J. Cohen
Graduate School of Industrial Administration
Carnegie Institute of Technology

Budget Control and Cost Behavior
Andrew C. Stedry
Graduate School of Industrial Administration
Carnegie Institute of Technology

The Structure of a Retail Market and the Market Behavior of Retail Units
Bob R. Holdren
Department of Economics
Yale University

Polya Type Distributions in Renewal Theory, with an Application to an Inventory Problem
Frank Proschan
Department of Statistics
Stanford University

The many high-quality dissertations submitted were judged by the most exacting professional standards. Specific criteria included:

a. Importance of the problem and originality of approach;
b. Use of the most appropriate and powerful tools of analysis;
c. Clear relation to the relevant theoretical framework or a contribution to theory;
d. Direct relevance to the practice of business or management;
e. Clarity and effectiveness of presentation.

An examination of all five volumes in this series will reveal that four of the five make considerable use of mathematical and statistical tools. This reflects the increasing importance of modern quantitative methods in the study of business. On the other hand, the use of quantitative techniques should certainly not be considered a *sine qua non* of rigorous research in business. It is hoped that in future years it will be possible to select for publication a greater number of nonmathematical dissertations of the highest quality.

On behalf of The Ford Foundation, I wish to express my sincere appreciation to the Editorial Committee for its painstaking effort in selecting the winning dissertations. The scholars who served as members of the Committee for the first year's competition were Robert Ferber, Research Professor of Economics, University of Illinois; Sherman J. Maisel, Professor of Business Administration, University of California (Berkeley); and William Foote Whyte, Professor, New York State School of Industrial and Labor Relations, Cornell University.

The work of the Editorial Committee was materially aided by a group of six readers, who spent hundreds of hours in conscientious examination of the dissertations submitted. The Foundation and the Committee wish to thank Professors Austin C. Hoggatt and Julius Margolis of the University of California (Berkeley), Henry A. Landsberger and Seymour Smidt of Cornell University, and Vernon K. Zimmerman and Thomas A. Yancey of the University of Illinois for their service as readers in the first year of the competition.

Finally, my colleagues and I wish to acknowledge the substantial contribution of Prentice-Hall, Inc., to the publication and distribution of the selected dissertations.

THOMAS H. CARROLL
VICE PRESIDENT
THE FORD FOUNDATION

New York, New York
January, 1960

Preface

This study was carried out as part of the research of the Organizational Behavior and Human Relations Program of the Institute for Social Research. I am grateful for the opportunity to work on this study while performing my regular duties as a member of this program and to use the facilities of the Institute.

I owe a great deal to Professors John Atkinson and John R. P. French, who gave freely of their time to discuss questions of psychological theory. I am also grateful for the assistance of the other members of my committee and particularly to my chairman, Floyd C. Mann.

For their continued help in the countless tasks involved in completing this dissertation I shall always be deeply indebted to Ellen Landau and Sandra Gratz. They have assisted me in matters of organization, style, and in other ways too numerous to mention.

Finally, I wish to acknowledge the contribution of my wife, Ann Vroom, whose interest and encouragement made the preparation of this dissertation very much easier.

VICTOR H. VROOM

Contents

ix

CHAPTER 4

ABILITY AND MOTIVATION   50

CHAPTER 5

DISCUSSION AND CONCLUSIONS   60

APPENDIX I

THE MEASURES   75

APPENDIX II

APPENDIX III

APPENDIX IV

BIBLIOGRAPHY

SOME
PERSONALITY DETERMINANTS
OF THE EFFECTS OF PARTICIPATION

CHAPTER 1

Introduction

Psychologists have long realized the importance of both environmental and personality variables in the explanation of behavior. Theorists have employed a variety of terms to describe the necessity of using both sets of concepts. Lewin, for example, illustrates this dual focus in his statement that "behavior (B) is a function (F) of the person (P) and of his environment (E), $B = F(P, E)$." (19)

However, there has been a tendency for researchers in social psychology to concentrate on one or the other of these sets of variables in their explanation of social phenomena. Some emphasize personality, conceived as the relatively enduring psychological properties of an individual, as the locus of the basic causes of behavior, while others look to environmental variables such as group structure, communication, and role. Few researchers investigate environmental and personality determinants of behavior simultaneously.

The situation in the field of industrial psychology is much the same. One major approach involves the prediction of an individual's job performance from a knowledge of his aptitudes, interests, and personality. Here the researchers are cognizant of the importance of environmental variables (e.g., the nature of the work performed) but make little attempt to treat them conceptually or use them as variables in prediction.

A second approach to the field of industrial psychology stresses environmental variables in the prediction of job performance. Historically this approach involved the determination of the effects of temperature, rest pauses, ventilation, and lighting on the performance of workers. More recently, however, the conception of work environment has broadened to include social aspects such as supervisory practices and group norms.

In both social and industrial psychology there has been a general reluctance to deal with personality and environmental variables simultaneously. As a result, while much is known about the separate effects of the two types of variables, little is known about the nature of their interaction. The need for research directed at this type of problem and for a theoretical framework capable of dealing with both personality and environmental variables is, however, widely recognized.

Katz has recently discussed the significance of this problem for social psychology:

> In other words, we have perpetuated the old dichotomy of approaches: either all individuals are affected similarly by group conditions or all group effects are explained as the expression of personality mechanisms. If social psychology has any unique subject matter, it may well lie in this neglected area of the interaction effects of personality and social settings. (14, p. 352)

Cronbach reached a similar conclusion in his recent presidential address before the American Psychological Association:

> In both applied work and general scientific work, psychology requires combined, not parallel, labors from our two historic disciplines. In this common labor, they will almost certainly become one, with a common theory, a common method, and common recommendations for social betterment. In the search for interactions we will invent new treatment dimensions and

discover new dimensions of the organism. We will come to
realize that organism and treatment are an inseparable pair
and that no psychologist can dismiss one or the other as error
variance. (8, p. 683)

The implications of this point of view for problems of leadership have been described by a number of writers (12). The
general conclusion is that leadership cannot be regarded as a
unitary trait and must be evaluated in terms of a number of
other variables including the attitudes, needs, and expectations
of the followers. The most effective behavior in dealing with
individuals with certain personality characteristics may be completely ineffective in dealing with persons with different personalities.

A similar point is made by those who argue for the adaptive
nature of leadership. After reviewing research on the effectiveness of different methods of supervision in industry, Likert
reached the following conclusion:

> Supervision is, therefore, always an adaptive process. A
> leader, to be effective, must always adapt his behavior to
> fit the expectations, values, and interpersonal skills of those
> with whom he is interacting. (21, p. 327)

The "authoritarian-democratic continuum" represents one aspect of leadership which has received much attention. In dis-
cussing studies dealing with this dimension Krech and Crutchfield
suggest that its effects may vary from culture to culture, as
follows:

> All the experimental evidence to be reported has been obtained
> by the study of so-called "authoritarian" and "democratic"
> leadership situations *in our democratic culture*. It is entirely
> possible that similar studies in other cultures might yield dif-
> ferent results. The advantage for morale, the experiments
> find, seem to lie with the democratically led group, but in an
> autocratic culture the reverse might possibly hold true. (15,
> p. 423)

Despite frequent speculations that the superior effects of democratic leadership are specific to certain personality types or cultures this problem has been virtually unexplored. The major purpose of the present study is to determine whether the effects of one aspect of the democratic leadership process—participation in decision-making—vary with the personality structure of the follower. The general hypothesis states that there is an interaction between those environmental conditions which are associated with participation and certain personality characteristics of the participant. Consequently, the effects of each variable can be understood best through the simultaneous study of both.

A secondary purpose of this study is to examine the relationship between ability and motivational variables in the determination of job performance.

1.1. Relevant Research

Most of the research on participation and related concepts has focused on a demonstration of their basic effects. Participation has been found to be related to such dependent variables as morale, productivity, turnover, and job satisfaction. Little research has been conducted, however, on the personality factors of the participant which influence these relationships.

Intimately related to amount of participation in decision-making is the democratic–authoritarian dimension of leadership, the pioneer study of which was carried out by Lewin, Lippitt, and White (20). They investigated the effects of authoritarian, democratic, and laissez-faire styles of leadership on the behavior of children organized into groups for the purpose of making masks. The democratically led groups were found to show less apathy, less aggression, and more group unity than the other two types of groups. While the general pattern of results favored the democratic leadership condition, Lewin, Lippitt, and White discovered two different types of reactions to the authoritarian condition. One reaction was clearly passive and dependent in nature, while the other was characterized by considerable aggression toward the leader. The authors attribute these differences to the personalities of the boys and to the order in which they experienced the different styles of leadership.

While individual differences in reaction to a single leadership pattern were most obvious in the authoritarian condition, there is some indication of diverse reactions to the democratic and laissez-faire styles. Most notable is the authors' description of one boy, the son of an army officer, who found a democratic atmosphere as frustrating as others had found the authoritarian atmosphere.

Similar concepts of leadership were used in a more recent study by Baumgartel (5). He divided laboratory chiefs in a scientific organization into directive, participative, and laissez-faire groups, depending on their predominant style of leadership. Participative leadership was associated with substantially higher motivation and more positive attitudes toward the leader than either of the other two styles. This study did not attempt to explain individual differences in reactions to the various leadership styles.

F. H. Sanford's study (36) sheds some light on this problem. He found that authoritarian personalities prefer status-laden leadership, accept strongly directive leadership, and regard the authoritarian leader as more effective than his democratic counterpart. Equalitarian personalities, on the other hand, accept authoritarian leadership only as the circumstances demand it.

Closely allied to the concept of participation is Lewin's concept of group decision. Lewin (18) used this term to refer to a group discussion along with individual decisions concerning action. A number of behaviors have been studied and found to be affected by such a process. These behaviors include industrial productivity (7, 16), food habits (33, 37), amount of halo effect in merit rating (17), and volunteering as subjects for experiments (6). While methods and results have varied somewhat from one study to another, the general pattern of findings indicates the value of group decision as a method for changing behavior and as a theoretical construct.

In a recent study on group decision Bennett (6) attempted to determine which aspects of the process are important in producing its experimental effects. She isolated four variables: group discussion, decision, commitment, and degree of consensus, all of which are involved in the Lewinian process of group decision. Her results suggest that the factors of group discussion and public commitment do not affect the probability that group members will execute the decision. The other two factors, the process of making a decision and the degree to which group consensus is obtained, were found to account for variations in the effectiveness of different techniques. In the light of these findings Bennett proposes that " 'group decision' might profitably be redefined as 'decision about individual goals in a setting of shared norms regarding such goals'." (6, p. 272)

Maier (22, 24) has demonstrated that the effects of group participation on the solution of group problems are not confined to the "acceptance of decisions" by group members and their subsequent motivation to carry them out. He has shown that leaders trained in group decision techniques can greatly improve the quality of a group's thinking by stimulating group members to more inventive solutions to problems.

Another related concept, used by Morse and Reimer to describe the role of various organization levels in decision-making, is that of locus of "organizational control." In a large-scale field experiment in an industrial setting they set out to test hypotheses concerning the role of rank and file employees in decision-making and individual satisfaction and productivity. The experimental design is summarized by the authors as follows:

> Using four parallel divisions of the clerical operations of an organization, two programs of changes were introduced. One program, the Autonomy program involving two of the divisions, was designed to increase the role of rank-and-file employees in the decision-making processes of the organization.

The other two divisions received a program designed to increase the role of upper management in the decision-making processes (the Hierarchically-controlled program). (30, p. 129)

As they had predicted, Morse and Reimer found that the satisfaction of employees increased in the Autonomy program and decreased in the Hierarchical program. Both programs, however, significantly increased productivity, with the Hierarchically-controlled program resulting in the greater increase. The difference between the two programs was not significant.

As part of the same experiment Tannenbaum investigated the role of personality factors in determining adjustment to the two experimental programs, one permitting workers greater opportunities for decision-making and the other restricting existing activities. Using paper and pencil personality tests, he obtained scores representing the strength of various personality trends and classified individuals on the basis of the estimated suitability of their personality structures to each of the experimental programs. It was found that persons "suited" to the program in which they were placed wanted their respective programs to last longer and were more satisfied than persons who were less suited to the program structure in which they were placed. Tannenbaum concludes that "social systems cannot be fully evaluated without an understanding of the psychological make-up of the individuals participating in that system." (38, p. 222)

In other relevant studies amount of participation in decision-making or conceptually similar variables was found to be related to attitudes toward foremen and shop stewards (13), turnover (34, 41), concern with costs (27), and absences (26). All of these studies focused on the average effects of participation without attempting to explain individual differences.

One of the more recent experiments was designed to investigate the possibility that cultural or individual variables have an important influence on the effects of participation. In a study carried out in a Norwegian factory, French, Israel, and Ås (10) obtained over-all results similar to those obtained in this country. They found, however, that the response of workers to participation was influenced by whether or not the worker felt that the participation was "legitimate." Legitimacy is defined as the extent to which participation is considered right and proper by the parties involved. Workers who felt that their participation was legitimate were more favorably affected by this experience than those who felt that their participation was not legitimate.

In summary, our review of the literature has shown considerable evidence for a number of behavioral consequences of participation and other democratic processes. Participation has been found to be related to a wide number of dependent variables including attitudes, absences, productivity, morale, and turnover. There has been relatively little research, however, on personality variables which interact with participation. The research which has been conducted on this problem has produced positive results. The task remains to determine the nature of the personality variables and the manner of their interaction with participation.

1.2. Concepts and Hypotheses

Participation. Many concepts have been used to describe democratic processes. There are, however, some differences in these concepts and in the ways each has been used by different researchers. It will be helpful to consider three of them, democratic leadership, group decision, and participation, in more detail before proceeding to a definition of participation for this study.

Democratic leadership is one of the more general of these concepts. It has usually been used to refer to a number of leader activities, the central one of which is involving group members in decision-making. Other activities sometimes included are working with the group and objectivity in praise and criticism.

Although the term "group decision" has been used widely, investigators do not agree on the specific leadership processes subsumed by the concept. In most of the studies conducted by

Lewin and his students, "group decision" refers to a group discussion accompanied by individual decisions about future action. The topic of the discussion is primarily of relevance to persons as individuals rather than as group members, and the decision represents a commitment to carry out a particular action proposed by the group leader rather than a solution of a problem.

Maier (23), on the other hand, uses the term to refer to decisions made by group members on group problems. In addition, he views the discussion preceding the decision as involving the consideration of various possible courses of action in solution of a problem, rather than the setting of goals in a direction suggested by the group leader.

Participation, the independent variable in this study, has also been used in a number of ways and has seldom been clearly defined. Frequently it is used to refer to the degree to which a person takes part in a discussion or activity. An individual who takes an active part in interacting with others with respect to a given task is said to participate a great deal, while one who plays a more passive role does not participate to the same degree.

In the present study, we shall use a somewhat different definition of participation, one originally put forth by French, Israel, and Ås (10). It will be defined as a process of joint decision-making by two or more parties in which the decisions have future effects on those making them. The amount of participation of any individual will be the amount of influence he has on the decisions and plans agreed upon.

This conception of participation is somewhat more restrictive than either democratic leadership or group decision. It includes the central core of these two concepts without adding other properties which may have different psychological effects. In addition, the conception of amount of participation provides for the possibility that a leader may behave in different ways with different group members or that group members may vary in their influence in a group decision.

Although participation is defined in terms of influence in

joint decision-making, it should be distinguished from such concepts as influence and control. The latter terms are much more inclusive since they refer also to influence exerted in situations other than those involving joint decision-making. An autocratic leader, for example, might have considerable influence within an organization but might not participate in making decisions with superiors or subordinates.

We will distinguish between psychological participation, or the amount of influence an individual perceives he has on decision-making, and objective participation, or the amount of influence he actually does have on decision-making. If perception is accurate, the amount of psychological participation will equal the amount of objective participation. Frequently, however, they will differ due to the influence of processes such as the effects of needs on perception. Unless otherwise noted, the term participation will refer to psychological participation.

The present study will be concerned primarily with the amount of psychological participation of persons with their superiors. It should be noted, however, that the hypotheses to be stated would also be expected to apply to objective participation and to joint decision-making with persons in other role relationships with the participant.

It is possible to distinguish conceptually between opportunity to participate, which is clearly a property of the situation or environment, and the amount of participation, which is a response of the individual to that environment. The amount of disparity between these two variables will depend on factors such as the range of decisions over which participation is considered and the degree to which participation is legitimized by societal norms and values.

In this study we have been unable to measure the opportunity of a supervisor to participate in decision-making independently of the extent to which he has participated in decision-making in the past. The opportunity to participate would seem to be accorded to those persons who have taken advantage of it most often in the past. Therefore, the terms amount of participation and opportunity to participate will be used interchangeably in referring to the operations in the present study.

In the research described earlier in this chapter, participation was related to a large number of dependent variables, including productivity, motivation, morale, job satisfaction, and turnover. We will be concerned here with its effect on attitudes and motivation.

Attitudes. The attitude construct has played an important role in the development of social psychological theory. For purposes of the present study, we will use the definition put forth by Peak. She defines attitude as a "process which involves affect organized around a conceptual or perceptual nucleus." (32, p. 152)

Theories concerning the determinants of attitudes usually emphasize the need-satisfying properties [1] of objects toward which the attitudes are held. If a physical or social object is rewarding to a person, he will develop a positive attitude toward it; if the object frustrates the person, he will develop a negative attitude toward it.

According to this theory, participation in decision-making will affect attitudes toward objects insofar as it affects the need-satisfying properties of these objects. If participation in decision-making satisfies important needs, then it will lead to more positive attitudes toward those objects or persons which are perceived to be instrumental in making participation possible. The affected attitudes will not be confined to those specific objects or persons involved in the participation process but may be expected to generalize to other objects and persons which are similar or closely associated. Thus, participating in a decision with one

---

[1] Various terms have been used to refer to these properties including instrumentality (32) and relevance (38).

representative of management is likely to have some effect on attitudes toward other members of management. Similarly, participating in a decision about a specific change in work method is likely to have some effect on attitudes toward work changes in general.

We will be concerned here with a more general orientation to the work situation. We shall term this variable "attitude toward the job." "Job" is used here in a broad sense to refer not only to the tasks which the individual performs, but also to his work relationships with other persons. The expected relationship between participation and attitude toward the job is stated in Hypothesis I.

Hypothesis I. The more an individual participates in making decisions on his job, the more positive will be his attitude toward that job.

Motivation. As G. Allport (2) has shown, most contemporary motivation theorists are still profoundly influenced by the hedonistic notion, dating back to the Greek philosophers, that behavior is guided by an attempt to maximize pleasure and minimize pain. Today this approach to behavior theory takes many forms. Freud's pleasure principle has been supplemented by more systematic concepts such as reinforcement, tension reduction, and restoration of equilibrium. While theorists differ in their conceptions of the motives, needs, or instincts underlying human action, they agree with one another in their assumption that, in any given situation, an individual will tend to select those responses which have been most satisfying in the past or are expected to lead to the greatest present satisfaction.

This view suggests that participating in making decisions would affect the motivation of an individual to the extent that it changes the amount of satisfaction or dissatisfaction that he expects as a result of performing various responses. The rationale for assuming that participation would have these effects has seldom been spelled out. Researchers have related participation to a large number of behaviors without specifying the process by which it accomplishes its effects.

French *et al.* (10) have carried out one of the more detailed analyses of the participative process. Working within a Lewinian framework, they hypothesize that participation in decision-making will motivate the participant to carry out the decision by increasing the "own forces" and decreasing the resistance forces acting in this direction. In other words, participation increases the expected satisfaction and decreases the expected dissatisfaction resulting from carrying out the decision.

The findings on group decision, as well as other studies relating participation to productivity, support this hypothesis. It should be noted, however, that the effects of participation in decision-making on any behavior depend on the relationship of that behavior to the decisions. Those behaviors which are instrumental to or consequences of carrying out the decision will be most affected. Therefore, productivity is more likely to be increased by participation in relevant decisions concerning the job, e.g., work methods and production goals (27).

Participating in a wide range of decisions of varying relevance to productivity may be expected to affect the general motivation for effective performance of the participant. In this case amount of participation is a function of both the number of joint decisions and the average amount of influence in these decisions. The expected relationship between participation and motivation is stated in Hypothesis II.

Hypothesis II. The more an individual participates in decision-making on his job, the greater will be his motivation for effective performance in that job.

It should be noted that motivation for effective performance is not the only variable mediating the effects of participation on productivity. As Maier (22, 23, 24) has pointed out, objective participation may lead to higher quality plans and decisions which may in themselves be reflected in performance.

Personality. Our major concern is to determine the influence of personality structure on the effects of participation. Although the development of theoretical formulations capable of dealing with both environmental and personality variables is quite limited, there is some theoretical basis for assuming that the effects of environment on attitudes and motivation would depend on personality.

Tannenbaum (38), for example, hypothesizes that an attitude toward an object is a multiplicative function of the strength of personality trends and the relevance of the object to the expression of these trends. The multiplicative nature of this formulation implies that the effects of variations in the relevance of an environmental object on a person's attitude toward the object vary with the strength of the personality trend. If the personality trend has a value of 0, there would be no relationship between the relevance of the object to that trend and attitude toward the object. Assuming that other factors also affect the attitude, it follows that as the strength of the trend increases, the effects of relevance on the attitude will also increase. Thus, expressing one variable as a multiplicative function of two other variables implies a particular form of interaction between the latter variables.

Other theorists have also used multiplicative models to describe the interaction between personality and situational variables. Peak (32) hypothesizes that attitudes toward objects are multiplicative functions of the intensity of values and the instrumentality of the objects with respect to these values. Atkinson (3), Tolman (40), and others have expressed motivation as a joint multiplicative function of motives or drives, which represent attributes of personality, and both incentive and expectancy, which represent intervening variables mediating the effects of situation or environment on behavior.

All of these theories would predict interactions between situational and environmental variables in the determination of attitudes and motivation. They do not provide much help, however, in selecting personality variables which might interact with participation. For assistance in this task it is necessary to turn to other aspects of psychological theory.

Need for independence and related concepts has appeared in the writings of many theorists. Freud (11) and other psycho-analytic theorists have emphasized the conflicting needs for independence and dependence involved in relationships with authority. The strong dependency needs developed in early relationships with authority conflict with needs for self-expression and provide the basis for ambivalent attitudes toward persons in positions of authority. This ambivalence explains why feelings of admiration for leaders often change quickly to rejection and hostility.

Murray (31) includes in his classification of personality variables the concept of need for autonomy. He uses this term to refer to the strength of a tendency to rebel against or defy authority. The individual who is high in need autonomy is described by Murray as "independent, free, willful, unrestrained, irresponsible."

McGregor has discussed the significance of need for independence in relation to problems of leadership. He distinguishes between two forms of expression of this need: active independence, which is "constructive and healthy," and reactive independence, which leads to "friction and strife." The character of the work environment determines which of these two tendencies is manifest in any individual. Under conditions of security and opportunity for growth and development, individuals will display active independence. On the other hand, reactive independence, in which the individual "will fight blindly for freedom," develops "if [he] feels that his dependence on his superiors is extreme, and if he lacks security." (29, p. 151)

McGregor points to participation in decision-making as an

important means for directing the need for independence into constructive channels.

> One of the most important conditions of the subordinate's growth and development centers around his opportunities to express his ideas and to contribute his suggestions before his superiors take action on matters which involve him. Through participation of this kind he becomes more and more aware of his superiors' problems, and he obtains a genuine satisfaction in knowing that his opinions and ideas are given consideration in the search for solutions. (29, p. 152)

While McGregor seems to regard need for independence as a general characteristic which has implications for effective leadership, he does acknowledge individual differences in the strength of this need.

> There are vast individual differences in tolerance for the inevitable pressures and insecurities attendant upon the acceptance of responsibility. Some subordinates seem to be content to achieve a high degree of security without independence. Others thrive on the risks and the dangers of being "on their own." (29, p. 152)

Following this lead of McGregor's, the present study will utilize need for independence as one of the personality variables which determine the effects of participation in decision-making. We shall define this variable as a predisposition to strive for self-reliance, to do things alone without help.

Our general hypothesis, which will be elaborated later in this chapter, is that persons with high need for independence would be more satisfied with and more motivated by situations which permit participation in decision-making than those with lower need for independence.

The concept of the authoritarian personality might also be relevant for predicting responses to different types of leadership. Adorno, *et al.* (1), report that highly authoritarian persons are characterized by a tendency toward submission to parents and authority figures. Equalitarian [1] persons, on the other hand, are able to express disagreement with parents and are able to achieve a greater amount of independence from them.

Sanford's (36) findings, reported earlier, give further support to the notion that authoritarian and equalitarian persons are differentially affected by certain leadership styles. On the basis of these and previous research findings one would predict that equalitarian persons would be more positively affected by participation in decision-making than authoritarian persons.

Hypotheses III and IV are concerned with the effects of participation on attitude toward the job for persons with different needs for independence and degrees of authoritarianism.

Hypothesis III. The stronger an individual's need for independence, the greater the extent to which participation in decision-making in his job will result in his developing a more positive attitude toward that job.[2]

Hypothesis IV. The more authoritarian the individual, the less the extent to which participation in decision-making in his job will result in his developing a more favorable attitude toward that job.[2]

Hypotheses V and VI make similar predictions concerning the effects of participation on motivation for effective performance.

Hypothesis V. The stronger an individual's need for independence, the greater the extent to which participation in decision-making in his job will increase his motivation for effective performance in that job.[2]

---

[1] The terms equalitarian and low authoritarian will be used synonomously.

[2] It should be noted that negative effects of participation on the attitudes and motivation of highly authoritarian persons, and persons with low need for independence are consistent with our theory. Our hypotheses are specific with respect to the direction of the difference in effects of participation but not concerning the absolute nature of these effects on the aforementioned groups.

Hypothesis VI. The more authoritarian the individual, the less the extent to which participation in decision-making in his job will increase his motivation for effective performance in that job.[1]

In Chapter 2 we will describe the field setting in which the research was carried out and the methods used to measure the variables. The findings concerning participation and personality will be reported in Chapter 3. In Chapter 4 we will analyze a related problem—the effects of ability and motivation on job performance. Finally, the implications of both sets of findings for theory and for future research will be discussed in Chapter 5.

---

[1] See Footnote 2, page 17.

CHAPTER 2

Methodology

2.1. Description of the Research Site

This study was carried out as part of an experiment[1] in a large company whose basic function is the delivery of small parcels and packages from department and other retail stores to private residences. The stores contract with the company to handle all their home deliveries in lieu of the stores' performing this function for themselves. This delivery service is offered in thirteen cities, the two largest of which are New York and Chicago, which were chosen as sites for the present study.

From its beginnings on the West Coast over 50 years ago, the company has become a major enterprise in the delivery business. In recent years it has expanded into two new kinds of operations —wholesale delivery and a city-to-city air service. Wholesale delivery involves the pickup and delivery of small parcels from the supplier to the business purchaser. The air service is a city-to-city wholesale and retail pickup and delivery service competing with Air Parcel Post and other rapid delivery services.

---

[1] This experiment was directed by Dr. Floyd Mann. It is one of a series of studies carried out within the Survey Research Center of the University of Michigan as part of its program of research on organizational behavior and organizational change.

While these lines initially represented only a small proportion of total volume, they are now expanding very rapidly and have created throughout the company the feeling that the organization is only midway in its expansion potential.

The delivery operation in each of the thirteen cities is called a plant and is headed by a plant manager. It is the company's policy to decentralize the management to the plants insofar as it is possible. Among the more specific functions allocated to each plant are the following: picking up parcels from retail and wholesale merchants, sorting parcels by geographic area (routes), assigning loads of parcels to particular trucks, delivering parcels to residences and business places, maintaining accurate and adequate financial and delivery records, dealing with problems arising from stores and buyers, carrying out time studies, planning delivery routes, employing new personnel, negotiating with unions, and maintaining equipment.

The organizational structure of the larger plants can best be described by showing the organizational hierarchy in the delivery operation of both the New York and Chicago plants. There are five levels of supervision in each of these plants. They are:

1. Plant Manager

2. Delivery Superintendent

3. Division Manager

4. Station Manager

5. Day and Night Supervisors

This study is concerned most directly with division managers, station managers, and day and night supervisors, and our description will be restricted to these levels.

The division manager is in charge of the operation of from three to eight stations in one geographical area. He usually has an office in one of these stations but spends a considerable proportion of his time visiting the other stations and working with his station managers on problems involving equipment, personnel, work methods, and scheduling.

The major responsibility for the operation of a station rests with the station manager. His duties include the planning of delivery routes, assigning routes to drivers, training and disciplining drivers, and maintaining records of driver performance. In a typical station, the station manager has both a night and a day supervisor reporting to him.

The night supervisor has by far the greater responsibility of the two. He supervises the work of all of the night crew directly and is responsible for work assignment and training, as well as maintaining performance records. The duties of the day supervisor vary considerably from station to station. In some stations his responsibilities are mainly clerical, while in others he performs many of the functions of the station manager.

The task of sorting parcels and loading them onto trucks is handled by four to twenty positioners in each station. They work on one side of a conveyor belt and place parcels in bins according to their destination. Positioners are typically paid on a group incentive basis with the standard expressed in terms of a certain number of pieces per hour.

The actual delivery operation is carried out by fifteen to fifty drivers in each station. Drivers report to work at about 8:30 A.M., get their work assignments and leave with their day's loads. They are expected to stay out until all of their parcels are delivered and are paid on an individual piece rate basis.

2.2. The Pattern of Participation

Interviews with station managers in the two plants and elsewhere in the company made it apparent that there was considerable variation in the way supervisors at all levels worked with their subordinates. Some supervisors, for example, constantly sought the ideas and opinions of those working for them and encouraged suggestions concerning improvements in the job. Others were much less inclined to involve their men in decisions and expressed the feeling that sharing problems with subordinates was a sign of inadequacy.

Variations in participation practices existed not only between supervisors, but also within a single supervisor's relationships with his different subordinates. A division manager, for example, might look to one of his station managers for ideas much more than other station managers.

While there are some differences in the pattern of participation from one level to another, most joint decision-making takes place between two persons: a supervisor and one of his subordinates. Group meetings are held occasionally but are usually informational and not for purposes of decision-making.

There are a number of reasons for using this pattern. One of these is the different hours and work locations of persons reporting to the same supervisor. A station manager, for example, finds it difficult to meet with his day and night supervisors together when their hours do not overlap. Similarly, a division manager must bring together station managers whose stations are separated by as much as 30 miles.

A second factor contributing to man-man as opposed to man-group relationships is the nature of the organizational structure. The supervisors in this study are not staff specialists whose joint knowledge must be utilized in the solution of organizational problems. They are, instead, functionaries in a line organization with clearly delegated operating responsibilities and somewhat unique operating problems.

2.3. Description of the Sample

The subjects in this study were 108 first, second, and third line supervisors employed in April, 1957, in the New York and Chicago plants of a large delivery company. The breakdown of the sample by occupational level is shown in Table 1.

TABLE 1. OCCUPATIONAL LEVEL OF THE SAMPLE

Occupational Level	Number	Per cent
Division Manager	8	7.4
Assistant Division Manager	2	1.8
Station Manager	35	32.4
Night Supervisor	30	27.8
Day Supervisor	33	30.6
Total	108	100.0

It should be noted that our sample is not a random sample of supervisors in general or even of supervisors within this particular organization. Strictly speaking, our conclusions will have to be restricted to the two plants that were studied.

2.4. Description of the Measures

The measures used in this study were obtained from research questionnaires and from company records. Questionnaires consisting of 125 items were completed by supervisors in the two plants in April, 1957. Each supervisor was asked to sign his questionnaire but was assured that his answers were completely confidential. At the same time shorter questionnaires were completed by drivers and positioners, who were not required to sign their names.

In November, 1957, approximately seven months after the original administration, similar questionnaires were completed by both supervisory and nonsupervisory personnel. These data have been used in obtaining estimates of reliability of the measures.

Information obtained from the company records included both ratings of the job performance of supervisors and scores on various tests of aptitude and ability. The ratings were available on all but twelve of the supervisors. In each case the most recent annual rating was used. The tests had been administered to supervisors at the time of hiring as part of the company's normal selection procedure.

The various measures used to test the hypotheses are described below. Copies of most of these measures may be found in Appendix I.

Psychological Participation. This index is derived by summing the responses of each supervisor to four questions. Each of these questions, designed to measure the extent to which the individual feels that he influences joint decisions made with his superior, was answered by checking the most applicable alternative on a five-point scale. Scores ranging from one, representing low participation, to five, representing high participation, were assigned to each question and total scores obtained for each person by summing his scores for the four items.

The items used and their intercorrelations appear in Table 2. All of the correlations reported are Pearson product-moment correlation coefficients.

TABLE 2. RELATIONSHIP BETWEEN ITEMS IN PSYCHOLOGICAL PARTICIPATION INDEX *

	Q. 26	Q. 28	Q. 30
Q. 8 In general, how much say or influence do you have on what goes on in your station?	−.07	+.10	−.02
Q. 26 Do you feel you can influence the decisions of your immediate superior regarding things about which you are concerned?		+.26***	−.01
Q. 28 Does your immediate superior ask your opinion when a problem comes up that involves your work?			+.21**
Q. 30 If you have a suggestion for improving the job or changing the setup in some way, how easy is it for you to get your ideas across to your immediate superior?			

* The levels of confidence of correlation coefficients will be indicated throughout this report by the following scheme:
*** $P < .01$
** $P < .05$
* $P < .10$

The intercorrelations between the items used in the index are surprisingly low. However, the issue of how homogeneous items should be before they are combined is really a complex one. Homogeneity is not an end in itself but is important only as far as it contributes to the reliability and validity of the resulting score. High homogeneity among items reflects both high reliability and considerable overlap among items. Combination of such items yields a total score representing a single, narrowly defined type of test material. Low homogeneity on the other hand may be due to unreliability among items or to the fact that the items measure somewhat different things. To the extent that these items are conceptually related and represent variables which have similar effects, combination of the items into a single score will broaden the range or breadth of the resultant measure.

The test-retest reliability of this index over a seven-month period is .61 for 91 supervisors. When 14 supervisors who changed either their position or their superior during this period were removed from this group, the reliability coefficent increased to .63. The correlation for the transferees is .44.

Other Participation Measures. Certain questions in both supervisory and nonsupervisory questionnaires required the respondent to report on the amount of participation of other persons in the organization. Station managers, for example, were asked to rate the influence of their day and night supervisors on what goes on in the station. These ratings were called the *superior-reported participation* scores of the supervisors.

In addition drivers were asked to rate the amount of participation of both station managers and day supervisors; positioners were asked to rate night supervisors; and station managers were asked to rate division managers. These ratings were made in response to the question:

"How much influence does your _____ have on what goes on in the station?"

The scores obtained by this method will be termed *subordinate-reported participation*.

It should be noted that the single item used in both of the above measures was the only item in the psychological participation index found to have nonsignificant relationships with the other three. It was, however, the only available item which offered some possibility of measuring objective participation.

If it is assumed that the amount an individual participates in decision-making is in part a reflection of certain leadership characteristics of his superior, then still another measure of participation may be obtained by averaging the responses of others reporting to the same superior to the question:

"Do you feel that you can influence the decisions of your immediate superior regarding things about which you are concerned?"

For example, in this study a measure of what we call *peer-reported participation* for a given station manager is obtained by averaging the responses of the other station managers reporting to the same division manager. It should be noted, however, that this index is conceptually a property of the superior of the participant, and thus only indirectly related to what we have defined as participation.

Table 3 summarizes the sources from which the various participation measures are derived.

TABLE 3. SOURCES OF DATA CONCERNING
PARTICIPATION OF PERSONS IN VARIOUS OCCUPATIONAL LEVELS

Occupational Level	Psychological Participation	Superior-Reported	Subordinate-Reported	Peer-Reported
Division Mgrs.	Division Mgrs.	None	Station Mgrs.	None
Station Mgrs.	Station Mgrs.	None	Drivers	Station Mgrs.
Night Superv.	Night Superv.	Station Mgrs.	Positioners	Drivers
Day Superv.	Day Superv.	Station Mgrs.	Drivers	Drivers

The superior-reported, subordinate-reported, and peer-reported measures are useful only as far as they reflect objective participation. Although no direct measure of this latter variable is available, some indication of the construct validity of these three measures may be obtained by determining their interrelationships. To the extent that they are highly related, one might conclude that they are really measuring objective participation.

Table 4 shows the matrix of intercorrelations between all four participation measures. Only one of the six correlations (psychological vs. peer-reported) is significant. All of the others are close to zero, with one approaching significance in a negative direction.

TABLE 4. RELATIONSHIPS BETWEEN DIFFERENT MEASURES OF PARTICIPATION

	Superior-Reported	Subordinate-Reported	Peer-Reported
Psychological participation	.02 ($N = 61$)	—.09 ($N = 101$)	.29 ($N = 102$)***
Superior-reported participation		.07 ($N = 45$)	—.16 ($N = 59$)
Subordinate-reported participation			.01 ($N = 98$)

*** $P < .01$

There are a number of possible reasons for this lack of relationship. Only one item was used in the measurement of the superior-reported, subordinate-reported, and peer-reported measures. While this was one of four items making up the psychological participation index, it has a relatively low relationship with the other three. It seems likely that the correlations are attenuated by the fact that parallel items were not used in each measure. In addition, factors such as bias on the part of the rater, lack of knowledge, and errors of measurement may be operating further to reduce the correlations. Whatever the reasons may be, however, these results indicate that none of the participation indices may safely be regarded as measuring objective participation. While any one of the four indices may be a measure of this variable, there is no way of telling which one it is. Consequently, most of our attention in this study will be devoted to the effects of psychological participation. The analysis of the data using the other three measures will be presented in Appendix IV.

Attitude Toward the Job. The measure of attitude toward the job consists of three items pertaining to various aspects of the work situation. These items and their correlations are shown in Table 5.

TABLE 5. RELATIONSHIP BETWEEN ITEMS IN ATTITUDE TOWARD THE JOB INDEX

	Q. 10	Q. 21
Q. 6 How well do you like supervisory work?	.21**	.07
Q. 10 How much of a chance does your job give you to do the things that you are best at?		.25***
Q. 21 How good is your immediate superior in dealing with people?		

*** $P < .01$
 ** $P < .05$

Each of the questions calls for the respondent to check the most appropriate answer on a five-point scale. Scores of one to five were assigned to each question and a total score obtained by adding over the three questions.

The test–retest reliability of this index over a seven-month period was computed for 91 supervisors and found to be .66. When fourteen supervisors who had changed their superior or their position within the organization during this period were removed, the reliability coefficient was increased to .75. The reliability for the transferees was .06.

Need for Independence. The measure of need for independence used in this study consists of 16 questionnaire items. Some of these items refer to the frequency with which the subject regularly engages in independent behavior (e.g., "How often do you find that you can carry out other people's suggestions without changing them any?"), while others deal with the satisfaction that he gets from this behavior (e.g., "When you have a problem, how much do you like to think it through yourself without help from others?"). Most of the items making up this measure were taken from a questionnaire developed and used by Tannenbaum and Allport (39). Each item requires the subject to check one of five alternatives.

For other purposes a short form of the need for independence measure, consisting of only eight items, was developed through an item analysis. This short form was found to intercorrelate .86 with the total score.

In November of 1957, seven months after the original questionnaires were completed, additional questionnaires containing the short need for independence measure were administered to 90 of the same supervisors. The test–retest reliability for this short form was .61.

Appendix I indicates the items used in both long and short forms of the need for independence measure.

Authoritarianism. The degree of authoritarianism of the subjects is measured by responses to 25 items from Forms 40 and 45 of the *F* scale developed by Adorno, *et al.* (1). A number of studies have been carried out to determine the reliability of this scale. The average of the reliability coefficients reported by the original authors is .90.

In keeping with the rest of the questionnaire, subjects were asked to check their degree of agreement with each of the statements on a five-point scale, unlike the six-point scale usually used.

The intercorrelation between the authoritarianism and need for independence measures is $-.11$ for 107 subjects. When age, occupational level, and education are partialled out from this relationship, the correlation is changed to .02. This means that these two personality variables are relatively independent.

Motivation for Effective Performance. The strength of motivation for effective performance is measured through ratings of job performance. Ratings on twelve different aspects of job performance were completed by the immediate superior of the man being rated and one other person who was acquainted with his work. We may assume that ratings indicate the degree to which motivation and ability are expressed in competent performance. Some of these rating factors, however, appear from their definitions to be primarily motivational (e.g., drive), while others seem to reflect ability factors (e.g., knowledge of work).

The rating form is divided into two parts. The first part consists of ten sets of five statements, each describing some aspect of job behavior. The rater is asked to rank-order the statements in terms of the degree to which they describe accurately the man whose performance they are rating. A sample set of statements appears below.

1. Can handle delicate situations
2. Requires help in planning his work
3. A good judge of the capabilities of others
4. Skillful at making work assignments
5. Has not yet demonstrated that he can progress further

The rankings on the ten sets of statements are scored to yield two indices—*over-all performance* and *potential.*[1]

The second part of the form consists of ten factors, listed below. Ratings are made on a twenty-point scale.

1. *Over-all Results:*
   a. In terms of production, cost and quality.
   b. Degree to which *his* skill, *his* methods, and *his* efforts are responsible for the above results—good or bad.
2. *Planning and Organizing:* Resourcefulness. Work habits. Planning, organizing and distributing of work for both short and long range objectives.

---

[1] The actual scoring of these indices was carried out by personnel in the organization in which the research was conducted. The details of the scoring procedure were not available.

3. *Drive:* Getting things done and carrying work to a finish, either by himself or through others.
4. *Judgments:*
   a. Soundness of judgments about people and actions taken on the basis of straight thinking in relation to them.
   b. Soundness of decisions in relation to his work.
5. *Teaching:* Increasing the skills of his men, getting his ideas across, creating a willingness in others, recognizing and developing the capabilities of others.
6. *Knowledge of Work:* Knowledge of his job, its responsibilities, and helpful related work.
7. *Personality:* Effect on other people as a result of his disposition, tact, enthusiasm, appearance, etc. Ability to work with and through others.
8. *Summary Appraisal:* All things considered.

Abilities. Four ability tests were used: (1) Otis Intelligence Test, (2) Arithmetic Reasoning Test, (3) Nonverbal Reasoning Test, and (4) Classification Test. With the exception of the Otis Test, these measures were developed by management consultants specifically for use in this company. All four tests are part of a supervisory selection program and were actually used in the selection of many of the supervisors in the sample. As a result, the range of scores on all ability measures has been somewhat restricted.

2.5. Description of the Statistical Procedures

All hypotheses have been tested by relating measurements on one variable with simultaneous measurements on another. Pearson product–moment correlation coefficients have been used throughout to determine the degree of relationships between variables. It should be noted that the Pearson r assumes interval scales in the variables being related. Since this requirement is not met in this study the reader is cautioned against too strict an interpretation of the magnitude of individual correlations or the obtained levels of confidence.

In as much as the direction of results has been specified in our hypotheses, one-tailed tests of significance have been performed. In cases in which the findings are in a direction opposite to that predicted, a more exploratory approach was adopted and the significance of the relationships tested using two-tailed tests. The .05 level of confidence has been accepted as the basis for rejecting the null hypothesis; results at the .05 to .10 level of confidence will be indicated to suggest trends.

CHAPTER 3

Results

In this chapter we will first examine data relevant to the testing of our hypotheses concerning the effects of participation on persons' attitudes toward their jobs. The findings concerning participation and motivation for effective performance will then be presented. Finally, the results on both of these problems will be summarized.

3.1. Participation and Attitude Toward the Job

Hypotheses I, III, and IV concern the effects of participation in decision-making on attitudes toward the job. Hypothesis I states that participation in decision-making will result in more favorable attitudes toward the job. The other two hypotheses are more refined statements of this relationship. Hypothesis III states that the effects of participation on the development of favorable attitudes varies directly with the strength of the participant's need for independence, and Hypothesis IV states that these effects vary inversely with the degree to which the participant is authoritarian.

These hypotheses are tested first using the measure of psychological participation. The general effects of psychological partici-

pation on attitudes toward the job are determined by intercor-
relating our measure of the former variable with attitude toward
the job for the entire sample. Then the sample is broken down
into groups scoring high, moderate, and low on each of the
personality variables. Psychological participation is intercorre-
lated with attitude toward the job within each of these six groups
to determine the relative effects of participation on persons with
different personality characteristics.

TABLE 6. RELATIONSHIP BETWEEN PSYCHOLOGICAL PARTICIPATION AND ATTITUDE
TOWARD THE JOB FOR PERSONS WITH DIFFERENT PERSONALITY CHARACTERISTICS

	Number of cases	r
Total Group	108	.36***
1. High Need Independence	38	.55***
2. Moderate Need Independence	32	.31**
3. Low Need Independence	38	.13
diff (1, 3) $t = 2.04'$ $P = .02$		
diff (1, 2) $t = 1.20'$ $P = .12$		
diff (2, 3) $t = —'$ $P = —$		
4. High Authoritarian	34	.03
5. Moderate Authoritarian	34	.35**
6. Low Authoritarian	39	.53***
diff (4, 6) $t = 2.33'$ $P = .01$		
diff (4, 5) $t = 1.36'$ $P = .09$		
diff (5, 6) $t = —'$ $P = —$		

*** $P < .01$
** $P < .05$
' Indicates that the difference between correlations is in the predicted direction;
t ratios over 1.00 will be shown.

The data in Table 6 support all three of the hypotheses concerning the effects of psychological participation on attitude

toward the job. The correlation between these variables for all subjects is positive, confirming our prediction in Hypothesis I. Significant differences are found, however, between the magnitude of the correlations for the different personality groups. As predicted, the most positive relationships between psychological participation and attitude toward the job are found for high need for independence and low authoritarian persons. Both correlations are significant at the .01 level of confidence. The least positive relationships are found for the low need for independence and high authoritarian persons. Neither of these correlations is significantly different from zero. The differences between correlations for high and low groups on both personality variables are statistically significant.

The data are interpreted as meaning that the attitudes toward the job of low authoritarian persons and of persons with high independence needs are favorably affected by opportunities to participate in making decisions in their jobs. On the other hand, the attitudes of highly authoritarian individuals and of individuals with low independence needs are relatively unaffected by this experience.

Appendix III presents the same findings in different form. It shows mean scores on attitude toward the job for persons in the six different personality classifications with various amounts of psychological participation. Similar breakdowns of mean scores for the other hypotheses are also shown in Appendix III.

The use of the correlational methods of field studies instead of the more precise techniques of laboratory experimentation increases the possibility that the results may be attributable to such factors as restriction in variance or failure to control for relevant variables. In order to check on the first of these possibilities we computed the variance on both independent and dependent variables for each of the six personality classifications. These variances, which are shown in Appendix II, show some evidence of restriction of range within the moderate categories on both personality variables. The moderate need for independence group has least variance on psychological participation and attitude toward the job, and the moderate authoritarian group has least variance on psychological participation. The differences between the high and moderate need for independence groups and the low and moderate authoritarian groups on attitude toward the job reaches significance at the .05 level of confidence. These differences are not sufficient to account for the findings.

The effects of background factors were checked by partialling out the effects of age, education, and occupational level from the relationship between psychological participation and attitude toward the job for each of the personality groups. Table 7 shows

TABLE 7. RELATIONSHIP BETWEEN PSYCHOLOGICAL PARTICIPATION AND ATTITUDE TOWARD THE JOB FOR PERSONS WITH DIFFERENT PERSONALITY CHARACTERISTICS, WITH AGE, EDUCATION, AND OCCUPATIONAL LEVEL HELD CONSTANT

	Number of cases	r
Total Group	108	.27***
1. High Need Independence	38	.51***
2. Moderate Need Independence	32	.25*
3. Low Need Independence	38	—.04
diff (1, 3) $t = 2.40'$ $P < .01$		
diff (1, 2) $t = 1.15'$ $P = .12$		
diff (2, 3) $t = 1.15'$ $P = .12$		
4. High Authoritarian	34	.09
5. Moderate Authoritarian	34	.35**
6. Low Authoritarian	39	.50***
diff (4, 6) $t = 1.77'$ $P = .04$		
diff (4, 5) $t = 1.04'$ $P = .15$		
diff (5, 6) $t = —'$ $P = —$		

*** $P < .01$
** $P < .05$
* $P < .10$
' In the predicted direction.

the third-order partial correlations (i.e., correlations between psychological participation and attitude toward the job with age, education, and occupational level held constant) for the six personality classifications.

Holding background factors constant serves to reduce most of the correlations very slightly. The magnitude of the differences between correlations, however, is slightly increased for need for independence and decreased for authoritarianism. All of the differences continue to be in the predicted direction, and the high-low differences on both variables meet our criterion of statistical significance.

The absence of relationship between need for independence and authoritarianism indicates that these variables are really independent of one another. It is possible, then, that greater differences in effects of participation may be obtained by using the two personality variables simultaneously. To test this we dichotomized the distributions on the two personality variables and computed the correlations between psychological participation and attitude toward the job for the four resulting groups.

Table 8 shows that the combined classification on both personality variables produces even greater differences in correlations. The correlation of .73 for the high need for independence and low authoritarian group indicates that more than 50 per cent of the variance on attitude toward the job is being accounted for in terms of amount of psychological participation. The difference between this group and the other three groups is significant at the .01 level or better. As would be expected, the lowest correlation is for the low need for independence and high authoritarian group.

These results suggest that participation in decision-making has a definitely favorable effect on the attitudes toward the job of low authoritarians who have a strong need for independence. On the other hand, high authoritarians with low need for independence are apparently unaffected by participating in making decisions. While there is no evidence of any negative effect of

TABLE 8. RELATIONSHIP BETWEEN PSYCHOLOGICAL
PARTICIPATION AND ATTITUDE TOWARD THE JOB FOR COMBINATIONS
OF NEED FOR INDEPENDENCE AND AUTHORITARIANISM

	Number of cases	r
1. High Need Independence and Low Authoritarian	29	.73***
2. High Need Independence and High Authoritarian	26	.25
3. Low Need Independence and Low Authoritarian	26	.12
4. Low Need Independence and High Authoritarian	26	.04

diff (1, 3)	$t = 2.79'$	diff (1, 4)	$t = 3.07'$	
	$P < .01$		$P < .01$	
diff (1, 2)	$t = 2.31'$	diff (2, 4)	$t = -'$	
	$P < .01$		$P = -$	
diff (2, 3)	$t = - +$	diff (3, 4)	$t = -'$	
	$P = -$		$P = -$	

*** $P < .01$
  ' In the predicted direction.
  + No direction was predicted for this difference.

participation on attitudes toward the job, the extent to which positive effects will result appears to be a function of the personality of the participant.

3.2. Participation and Motivation for Effective Performance

Hypotheses II, V, and VI concern the effect of participation in decision-making on participants' motivation to do well in their jobs. Hypothesis II is the frequently stated general proposition that participation in decision-making will increase employees' motivation for effective performance in their jobs. The other two hypotheses are refinements of this proposition stating that the positive effects of participation on motivation will vary directly with the strength of independence needs (Hypothesis V) and inversely with degree of authoritarianism (Hypothesis VI).

Although no direct measure of motivation for effective performance is available, it is assumed to be reflected in various ratings of job performance. The twelve rating factors which were discussed in the previous chapter vary considerably in the extent to which they appear, on the basis of their definitions, to reflect this motivation factor. Our hypotheses would predict greater differences between the correlations on factors reflecting motivation as opposed to ability. In the tables dealing with these relationships we will order the twelve rating factors roughly in terms of their expected relationship with motivation for effective performance.

Table 9 shows the intercorrelations between psychological participation and the twelve rating factors for the entire sample and for the high, moderate, and low need for independence subgroups. The factors are arranged from left to right in decreasing order of relevance to motivation. For purposes of discussion we may assume that the five rating factors on the left side of the page are primarily influenced by motivation while the remaining seven are primarily influenced by ability.

These findings support the hypothesis concerning the general effects of participation on motivation for effective performance. The correlations between psychological participation and six of the rating factors for the total group are statistically significant at the .05 level. Four of these factors are included in the group that we have called motivational.

In addition, some support is provided the hypothesis that the effects of participation on motivation are a function of the strength of the participant's need for independence. All twelve comparisons of high and low need for independence groups are in the expected direction. Five of the twelve correlations for the high group and only one of the correlations for the low group are significant at the .10 or .05 levels. None of the differences between correlations is significant, but there is a tendency toward significance among the first three rating factors, i.e., those most expected to reflect motivation.

The data in Table 10 demonstrate considerable support for

TABLE 9. RELATIONSHIP BETWEEN PSYCHOLOGICAL PARTICIPATION AND RATINGS OF JOB PERFORMANCE FOR TOTAL GROUP AND FOR PERSONS WITH HIGH, MODERATE, AND LOW NEED FOR INDEPENDENCE

Pearson r's between psychological participation and supervisor's ratings on:

	N	Drive	Over-all Performance	Summary Appraisal	Over-all results (a)	Over-all results (b)	Planning & Organizing	Teaching	Personality	Judgment (a)	Judgment (b)	Potential	Knowledge of work
Total Group	96	.15*	.20**	.20**	.22**	.20**	.28***	.12	.11	.17**	.11	.05	.15*
1. High Need Independence	33	.22	.33**	.25*	.31**	.20	.40**	.16	.16	.23	.11	.05	.26*
2. Moderate Need Independence	28	.29*	.19	.33**	.10	.31*	.12	.08	.16	.26*	.20	.22	—.03
3. Low Need Independence	35	.00	.06	—.01	.20	.12	.32**	.14	—.05	.00	.06	—.12	.16
diff (1,3) $t=$		—'	1.12'	1.08'	—'	—'	—'	—'	—'	—'	—'	—'	—'
$P=$		—	.13	.14	—	—	—	—	—	—	—	—	—
diff (1,2) $t=$		—	—'	—	—'	—	1.11'	—'	—	—	—	—	1.11'
$P=$		—	—	—	—	—	.13	—	—	—	—	—	.13
diff (2,3) $t=$		1.11'	—'	1.30'	—	—'	—	—	—'	—'	—	1.26'	—
$P=$		.13	—	.10	—	—	—	—	—	—	—	.10	—

*** $P < .01$
** $P < .05$
* $P < .10$
' In the predicted direction.

TABLE 10. RELATIONSHIP BETWEEN PSYCHOLOGICAL PARTICIPATION AND RATINGS OF JOB PERFORMANCE FOR HIGH, MODERATE, AND LOW AUTHORITARIAN PERSONS

					Pearson r's between psychological participation and supervisor's ratings on:								
	N	Drive	Over-all Perform-ance	Summary Appraisal	Over-all results (a)	(b)	Planning & Organ-izing	Teach-ing	Person-ality	Judgment (a)	(b)	Poten-tial	Know-ledge of work
1. High Authoritarian	30	-.16	-.08	-.06	-.11	.03	.04	-.06	-.10	.05	.21	-.18	.18
2. Moderate Authoritarian	33	.15	.28*	.23*	.38**	.17	.24*	.06	.18	.26*	.20	.08	.11
3. Low Authoritarian	32	.36**	.28*	.27*	.33**	.30*	.38**	.22	.17	.09	-.19	.06	.15
diff (1, 3) t =		2.00'	1.37'	1.26'	1.67'	—'	1.33'	—'	—'	—'	1.48	—'	—
P =		.02	.08	.10	.05	—	.09	—	—	—	.14	—	—
diff (1, 2) t =		1.19'	1.42'	1.12'	1.96'	—'	—'	—'	—'	—'	—	—'	—'
P =		.12	.08	.13	.03	—	—	—	—	—	—	—	—
diff (2, 3) t =		—'	—	—'	—	—'	—'	—'	—	—	1.50	—	—'
P =		—	—	—	—	—	—	—	—	—	.14	—	—

** $P < .05$
* $P < .10$
' In the predicted direction.

the hypothesized interaction between participation and authoritarianism in determining motivation for effective performance. The correlations between psychological participation and six of the rating factors are significant at the .10 level or better within the low authoritarian group. None of the correlations are significant at this level in the high authoritarian group.

As would be predicted the differences between correlations in the high and low groups are greatest in magnitude for the "motivational" rating factors. The differences on four of the five rating factors most expected to reflect motivation are significant at the .10 level or better. Only one of the high–low differences in the seven "ability" factors is significant at this level.

These findings suggest that the generalization concerning the positive effects of participation on motivation is an over-simplification. The general finding that participating in decisions increases motivation is only an average effect and obscures the fact that some persons are unaffected by the experience. An adequate theoretical explanation of these effects must consider the role of personality variables as they interact with participation.

The supplementary analyses applied to the findings relating participation to attitude toward the job were also carried out here. Appendix II shows the variance on two of the performance variables for each of the different personality groups. The slight differences which do exist are not statistically significant and cannot account for the findings.

Third-order partial correlations were also computed between psychological participation and two of the performance variables by controlling for the background characteristics of age, education, and occupational level. A comparison of Table 11 with Tables 9 and 10 shows that partialling out the effects of these variables generally increases the magnitude of the differences between correlations and provides further support for our hypotheses. All of the differences are in the predicted direction, and three of the four possible high–low comparisons are significant.

TABLE 11. RELATIONSHIP BETWEEN PSYCHOLOGICAL PARTICIPATION AND RATINGS
OF JOB PERFORMANCE FOR PERSONS WITH DIFFERENT PERSONALITY CHARACTERISTICS
WITH AGE, EDUCATION, AND OCCUPATIONAL LEVEL HELD CONSTANT

| | | Pearson r's between psychological participation and supervisor's ratings on: | |
	N	Over-all Performance	Summary Appraisal
Total Group	96	.21**	.20**
1. High Need Independence	33	.51***	.42**
2. Moderate Need Independence	28	.18	.33**
3. Low Need Independence	35	.04	.00
diff (1, 3) $t =$		1.93'	1.61'
$P =$		.03	.05
diff (1, 2) $t =$		1.31'	—'
$P =$		.10	—
diff (2, 3) $t =$		—'	1.26'
$P =$		—	.10
4. High Authoritarian	30	—.13	.14
5. Moderate Authoritarian	33	.24*	.18
6. Low Authoritarian	32	.33**	.26*
diff (4, 6) $t =$		1.68'	—'
$P =$		.05	—
diff (4, 5) $t =$		1.32'	—'
$P =$		.09	—
diff (5, 6) $t =$		—'	—'
$P =$		—	—

*** $P < .01$
** $P < .05$
* $P < .10$
' In the predicted direction.

Table 12 shows the correlations between psychological participation and job performance for groups classified on the basis of their scores on both personality variables. The differences in correlations are similar in magnitude to those shown in Tables 9 and 10 but are reduced in significance due to the smaller number of cases within each group. It seems likely that partialling out the effects of background factors would increase the differences and add further support to our findings.

TABLE 12. RELATIONSHIP BETWEEN PSYCHOLOGICAL PARTICIPATION AND JOB PERFORMANCE FOR COMBINATIONS OF NEED FOR INDEPENDENCE AND AUTHORITARIANISM

		Pearson r's between psychological participation and supervisor's ratings on:	
	N	Over-all Performance	Summary Appraisal
1. High Need Independence and Low Authoritarian	26	.34**	.34**
2. High Need Independence and High Authoritarian	24	.13	.11
3. Low Need Independence and Low Authoritarian	22	.03	.08
4. Low Need Independence and High Authoritarian	23	.12	.14
diff (1, 3) $\quad t =$		1.03′	—′
$\quad\quad\quad\quad P =$		.15	—
diff (1, 2) $\quad t =$		—′	—′
$\quad\quad\quad\quad P =$		—	—
diff (1, 4) $\quad t =$		—′	—′
$\quad\quad\quad\quad P =$		—	—
diff (2, 3) $\quad t =$		—+	—+
$\quad\quad\quad\quad P =$		—	—
diff (2, 4) $\quad t =$		—′	—
$\quad\quad\quad\quad P =$		—	—
diff (3, 4) $\quad t =$		—	—
$\quad\quad\quad\quad P =$		—	—

** $P < .05$
′ In the predicted direction.
+ No direction predicted.

The data reported in this section support the hypothesis that participation generally has positive effects on motivation for effective performance and the more specific hypotheses that the magnitude of these effects depends on the need for independence and authoritarianism of the participant. There are, however, at least two possible explanations for the participation-motivation relationship. The first of these explanations is based on the assumption that people enjoy carrying out decisions which they have helped to make. The more a person participates in making decisions the more positively motivated he is to carry out these decisions successfully.

This sort of explanation has been used by a number of researchers. Various terms have been used to describe the process. Maier (23) states that participation increases the ego-involvement of the individual in the decision. French, Israel and Ås (10), on the other hand, hypothesize that participation will increase the "own forces" on the person to carry out the decision.

The second explanation of the positive relationship between participation and motivation involves the effects of other decision-making processes which are characteristically associated with low participation. In an on-going organization decisions have to be made by one process or another. If a decision is not made in a participative manner, the chances are increased that it will be made unilaterally by a person in a position of authority. Consequently, lack of participation in decision-making is likely to be associated with being ordered to carry out decisions by one's superior. The relatively poor motivation of the person with low participation may be due, therefore, not to the fact that he doesn't participate, but to the fact that he is dominated by his superior. If it is assumed that people dislike carrying out orders from other persons, domination may be expected to result in negative motivation.

The data in the present study may shed some light on the relative validity of these two explanations. As we have noted above, the magnitude of the effect of participation on motivation is a direct function of the strength of independence needs and an inverse function of degree of authoritarianism. If the relationship between participation and motivation is due to the fact that participation creates only positive motivation for effective performance, then under high participation conditions we would expect persons with strong independence needs to perform better than persons with weaker independence needs. Similarly, low authoritarians would perform better than high authoritarians. Under low participation conditions there should be little or no difference in the performance of these groups.

On the other hand, if the relationship between participation and motivation is due to the fact that low participation is associated with domination and domination creates negative motivation, we would expect this negative motivation to be greatest in the case of high need for independence and low authoritarian persons. Under low participation conditions persons with weak independence needs would perform better than those with high independence needs, and high authoritarians would out-perform low authoritarians.

Tests of these alternative predictions have been carried out, and the results are presented in Table 13. Instead of controlling for personality, it was necessary to control for amount of participation and then intercorrelate personality characteristics with performance.

These findings provide some evidence for both propositions. As would be predicted from the proposition that participation increases positive motivation, under high psychological participation conditions the correlations between need for independence and the three performance variables are positive, and the correlations between authoritarianism and performance are negative. On the other hand, there is a tendency for a reversal in the direction of these relationships under low participation conditions. Five of the six correlations between personality and performance are in the direction predicted from the proposition that the apparent effects of participation on motivation are due to the negative effects of domination which is characteristically associated with low participation. The question of the confounding of the effects of participation with those of other decision-making processes will be explored in more detail in the last chapter.

TABLE 13. RELATIONSHIP OF NEED FOR INDEPENDENCE AND AUTHORITARIANISM WITH RATINGS OF JOB PERFORMANCE FOR PERSONS WITH HIGH, MODERATE, AND LOW PSYCHOLOGICAL PARTICIPATION

		Pearson r's between need independence and supervisor's ratings on:		
	N	Drive	Over-all Performance	Summary Appraisal
1. High Participation	30	.13	.39**	.25*
2. Moderate Participation	34	—.18	.38**	—.06
3. Low Participation	32	—.17	.05	—.04
diff (1, 3) $t =$		1.12′	1.34′	1.12′
$P =$		.13	.09	.13
diff (1, 2) $t =$		1.18′	—′	1.22′
$P =$		.12	—	.11
diff (2, 3) $t =$		—	1.35′	—
$P =$		—	.09	—

		Pearson r's between authoritarianism and supervisor's ratings on:		
	N	Drive	Over-all Performance	Summary Appraisal
1. High Participation	29	—.29*	—.20	—.04
2. Moderate Participation	34	—.05	—.36**	—.42**
3. Low Participation	32	.17	.08	.25*
diff (1, 3) $t =$		1.75′	1.04′	1.08′
$P =$		.04	.15	.14
diff (1, 2) $t =$		—′	—	1.56
$P =$		—	—	.12
diff (2, 3) $t =$		—′	1.78′	2.70′
$P =$		—	.04	.01

** $P < .05$
* $P < .10$
′ In the predicted direction.

3.3. Summary

The findings reported in this chapter may be summarized as follows:

1. A significant but low positive correlation was found between

amount of psychological participation and employees' attitudes toward their jobs. This result was regarded as giving support to our hypothesis that participation will, in general, lead to more favorable attitudes toward the job (Hypothesis I).

2. A correlation of similar magnitude was obtained between amount of psychological participation and over-all job performance. This result was interpreted as evidence for the hypothesized general effects of participation on motivation for effective performance (Hypothesis II).

3. Significantly different correlations were obtained between psychological participation and attitude toward the job for persons with high and low needs for independence. This finding substantiates our hypothesis that participation has more positive effect on the attitudes of those with strong independence needs (Hypothesis III).

4. Significant differences in correlation between psychological participation and attitude toward the job were also obtained for high and low authoritarian groups. This difference substantiates our hypothesis that participation is more satisfying to low than high authoritarians (Hypothesis IV).

5. Differences approaching significance were found between the correlations of psychological participation with ratings of job performance of persons with high, moderate, and low needs for independence. The greatest differences were found for those rating factors expected to be most sensitive to motivational influences. These differences are in the direction indicated by Hypothesis V which states that participation will have greatest effect on the motivation of persons with high independence needs.

6. Similar differences were found between the correlations of psychological participation and ratings of job performance for high, moderate, and low authoritarians. These differences support our hypothesis that low authoritarians will be more moti-

vated by participating in decision-making than high authoritarians (Hypothesis VI).

7. Partialling out the effects of age, education, and occupational level from correlations between psychological participation and both attitude toward the job and job performance generally serves to increase the differences between personality groups and lend further support to our hypotheses.

8. Categorizing persons on the basis of their scores on both need for independence and authoritarianism produced greater differences in correlations between psychological participation and attitude toward the job, but did not affect the correlations with job performance.

9. An examination of the correlations between the two personality variables and job performance under varying amounts of psychological participation showed both positive and negative correlations depending on the amount of participation. This finding was interpreted as meaning that the relationship between participation and performance is due both to the positive effects of participation on motivation for effective performance and to the negative effects of domination, which may be expected to be associated with the absence of participation.

CHAPTER 4

Ability and Motivation

4.1. Introduction

Up to now the focus has been on the interaction between participation and personality. Another interaction was also explored in the present study—that between ability and motivation variables in the determination of job performance. While ability and motivation have long been regarded as conceptually separable determinants of performance, their joint effects have seldom been studied. Traditionally the former variable has been within the province of psychologists interested in problems of selection and placement, while the latter has been studied most frequently by social psychologists interested in interpersonal relationships within organizations. Seldom have both ability and motivation been used together to predict performance. The implicit assumption seems to have been that the effects of each variable are independent and do not require simultaneous study.

Two studies of this problem do not support such an assumption. They both found interactions between ability and motivation in determining performance. Atkinson found that under "achievement-orienting" instructions the performance level of persons who were high in need Achievement was significantly higher than persons low in need Achievement on both number of attempted and number of correct solutions to arithmetic problems. This difference between high and low motivation groups was greater for persons having low scores on a Quantitative Aptitude Test than for persons with high scores. Although this finding was not statistically significant, it suggested, nevertheless, that "persons who are low in aptitude profit most by strong motivation." (4, p. 365)

In another study E. G. French investigated the interaction of intelligence and achievement motivation in determining problem solving success. Her hypothesis that "intelligence level is related to problem solving success among subjects with high achievement motivation but not among subjects with low achievement motivation" was confirmed. (9, p. 400) The difference between these results and those of Atkinson may be due in part to the different types of tasks used in the two studies. Atkinson used relatively simple arithmetic problems, while the tasks employed by French were more complex.

These findings suggest that there are important interactions between ability and motivation even though the nature of the interaction may depend on certain properties of the task.

The present study attempts to explore further the joint effects of motivation and ability. Instead of using laboratory tasks, our focus is on the effects of these variables on the performance of supervisors in an industrial organization.

Our hypothesis, which is taken from Maier (25), states that job performance is a multiplicative function of ability and motivation. According to this formulation the effects of ability on job performance should be directly proportional to strength of motivation. If motivation for effective performance is zero, there should be no relationship between ability and performance. As the strength of motivation increases, however, the relationship between ability and performance should become increasingly positive.

4.2. The Derived Motivation Measures

In the findings reported in the previous chapter we used ratings of job performance as our measure of motivation. Since we are interested in studying motivation as a determinant of job performance, it is necessary to obtain a measure of this variable which is operationally independent of performance.

The data shown in the preceding chapter indicate that the correlation between psychological participation and motivation becomes increasingly positive with increasing need for independence. While a number of mathematical formulas may be shown to fit these data, probably the simplest is a multiplicative function shown in the following equation:

$$M_{NI} = (NI \times P) + F$$

where
M_{NI} = derived motivation for effective performance based on need for independence
NI = strength of need for independence
P = amount of psychological participation
F = additional factors affecting motivation

The scores on need for independence and amount of psychological participation are multiplied, as in the above equation, in order to measure motivation for effective performance.[1]

A similar measure of motivation was obtained from authoritarianism scores and amount of psychological participation. Since our previous findings have shown the highest correlation between participation and motivation for low authoritarian persons and the lowest correlation for high authoritarian persons, a slight modification had to be introduced in the equation, as shown below:

---

[1] This index might also be used as a measure of attitude toward the job, since the above equation is applicable to the data on this variable.

$$M_A = [(K - A) \times P] + F$$

where

$M_A =$ derived motivation for effective performance based on authoritarianism

$K =$ the total possible authoritarianism score

$A =$ the individual's actual authoritarianism
score

$P =$ amount of psychological participation

$F =$ additional factors affecting motivation

4.3. Results

These two derived measures of motivation for effective performance will now be used to test our hypothesis concerning the
effects of ability on persons with differing levels of motivation.
To distinguish the two measures, we will use the symbol Motiva-
tion$_{(NI)}$ to represent motivation for effective performance based
on need for independence scores and Motivation$_{(Auth)}$ for the
measure based on authoritarianism scores. The procedure used
in test of this hypothesis was similar to that used in the preceding
chapter to determine the joint effects of participation and personality. The subjects were divided into three groups based on their
scores on each of the derived motivation indices and the correlation between various ability measures and performance determined within each group.

Tables 14–17 show the intercorrelations between scores on
the four ability tests and ratings of job performance for persons
with high, moderate, and low derived motivation for effective
performance$_{(NI)}$.

In general, the findings support our hypothesis. All of the
differences in correlations between high and low motivation
groups are in the predicted direction. Eleven out of sixteen of
these differences are significant at the .10 level and six differences
are significant at the .05 level.

While findings from all four of the ability measures tend to

TABLE 14. RELATIONSHIP BETWEEN OTIS INTELLIGENCE AND RATINGS OF JOB PERFORMANCE FOR HIGH, MODERATE, AND LOW DERIVED MOTIVATION(NI) PERSONS

		Pearson r's between Otis and:			
	N	Over-all Perform- ance	Summary Appraisal	Over-all Results (a)	Over-all Results (b)
1. High Motivation (*NI*)	33	.32**	.28*	.01	.01
2. Moderate Motivation (*NI*)	28	.22	.14	.10	.16
3. Low Motivation (*NI*)	31	—.09	—.09	—.34**	—.38*
diff (1, 3) $t =$		1.62'	1.46'	1.38'	1.58'
$P =$		.05	.07	.08	.06
diff (1, 2) $t =$		—'	—'	—	—
$P =$		—	—	—	—
diff (2, 3) $t =$		1.13'	—'	1.64'	2.04'
$P =$		.13	—	.05	.02

** $P < .05$
* $P < .10$
' In the predicted direction.

TABLE 15. RELATIONSHIP BETWEEN ARITHMETIC REASONING AND RATINGS OF JOB PERFORMANCE FOR HIGH, MODERATE, AND LOW DERIVED MOTIVATION(NI) PERSONS

		Pearson r's between Arithmetic Reasoning and:			
	N	Over-all Perform- ance	Summary Appraisal	Over-all Results (a)	Over-all Results (b)
1. High Motivation (*NI*)	31	.29*	.24*	.49***	.21
2. Moderate Motivation (*NI*)	28	—.10	.10	.24	.27*
3. Low Motivation (*NI*)	32	—.02	.02	—.13	—.15
diff (1, 3) $t =$		1.23'	—'	2.58'	1.38'
$P =$		.11	—	$<.01$	.08
diff (1, 2) $t =$		1.45'	—'	1.09'	—
$P =$		.07	—	.14	—
diff (2, 3) $t =$		—	—'	1.37'	1.59'
$P =$		—	—	.09	.06

*** $P < .01$
* $P < .10$
' In the predicted direction.

TABLE 16. RELATIONSHIP BETWEEN NONVERBAL REASONING AND RATINGS OF JOB
PERFORMANCE FOR HIGH, MODERATE, AND LOW DERIVED
MOTIVATION (NI) PERSONS

			Pearson r's between Nonverbal Reasoning and:			
		N	Over-all Perform- ance	Summary Appraisal	Over-all Results (a)	Over-all Results (b)
1. High Motivation (*NI*)		31	.47**	.56***	.33**	.21
2. Moderate Motivation (*NI*)		28	.06	—.04	—.19	—.05
3. Low Motivation (*NI*)		32	—.07	—.23*	—.17	—.31**
diff (1, 3)	$t =$		2.23'	3.31'	1.96'	2.04'
	$P =$		.01	<.01	.03	.02
diff (1, 2)	$t =$		1.63'	2.44'	1.93'	—'
	$P =$		.05	<.01	.03	—
diff (2, 3)	$t =$		—'	—'	—	1.00'
	$P =$		—	—	—	.16

*** $P < .01$
** $P < .05$
* $P < .10$
' In the predicted direction.

TABLE 17. RELATIONSHIP BETWEEN CLASSIFICATION TEST AND RATINGS OF JOB
PERFORMANCE FOR HIGH, MODERATE, AND LOW DERIVED
MOTIVATION (NI) PERSONS

			Pearson r's between Classification Test and:			
		N	Over-all Perform- ance	Summary Appraisal	Over-all Results (a)	Over-all Results (b)
1. High Motivation (*NI*)		31	.17	.20	.06	.19
2. Moderate Motivation (*NI*)		28	.30*	.22	—.06	—.07
3. Low Motivation (*NI*)		32	.01	—.15	—.09	—.01
diff (1, 3)	$t =$		—'	1.35'	—'	—'
	$P =$		—	.09	—	—
diff (1, 2)	$t =$		—	—	—'	—'
	$P =$		—	—	—	—
diff (2, 3)	$t =$		1.11'	1.37'	—'	—
	$P =$		.13	.09	—	—

* $P < .10$
' In the predicted direction.

substantiate our hypothesis, the strongest evidence comes from the Nonverbal Reasoning Test. All four of the high–low motivation$_{(NI)}$ differences are significant at the .05 level or better. Weakest support is found with the Classification Test in which only one of the high–low differences surpasses the .10 level of confidence.

The negative correlations between all four ability measures and performance for the low motivation group represent an unexpected finding. All but two of the sixteen correlations between the ability and performance measures are negative with three of them significant at the .05 level.

One possible explanation for this finding stems from the subjective source of the performance measures. Ratings of job performance may reflect in part the potential of the man being rated. A person of high ability who is performing far below his capacity may receive a lower rating than a man of lesser ability who is performing at the same level. This effect would serve to reduce all correlations between ability measures and ratings of performance and account for negative correlations in low motivation groups.

Negative correlations might also be due to motivational variation within the low motivation group. Persons high in ability who are in the low motivation group might be frustrated due to the fact that they are unable to make use of this ability. Such frustration might constitute an additional force toward low performance which would not be experienced by those with less ability.

Tables 18–21 show the intercorrelations between the ability and performance for high, moderate, and low derived motivation$_{(Auth)}$ persons.

These findings show little support for our hypothesis. Although ten out of sixteen of the high–low motivation differences are in the predicted direction, few of them approach significance. The greatest difference in correlations is found with the Otis

TABLE 18. RELATIONSHIP BETWEEN OTIS INTELLIGENCE AND RATINGS OF JOB PERFORMANCE FOR HIGH, MODERATE, AND LOW DERIVED MOTIVATION(AUTH) PERSONS

			Pearson r's between Otis and:			
		N	Over-all Perform- ance	Summary Appraisal	Over-all Results (a)	Over-all Results (b)
1. High Motivation (Auth)		30	.36**	.19	—.07	—.08
2. Moderate Motivation (Auth)		29	.26*	.46***	.17	.23
3. Low Motivation (Auth)		32	—.11	—.09	—.28*	—.29*
diff (1, 3)	$t =$		1.81'	1.04'	—'	—'
	$P =$		.04	.15	—	—
diff (1, 2)	$t =$		—'	1.15	—	1.15
	$P =$		—	—	—	—
diff (2, 3)	$t =$		1.41'	2.18'	1.70'	1.96'
	$P =$		.08	.02	.04	.03

*** $P < .01$
** $P < .05$
* $P < .10$
' In the predicted direction.

TABLE 19. RELATIONSHIP BETWEEN ARITHMETIC REASONING AND RATINGS OF JOB PERFORMANCE FOR HIGH, MODERATE, AND LOW DERIVED MOTIVATION(AUTH) PERSONS

			Pearson r's between Arithmetic Reasoning and:			
		N	Over-all Perform- ance	Summary Appraisal	Over-all Results (a)	Over-all Results (b)
1. High Motivation (Auth)		28	.04	.05	.34**	.10
2. Moderate Motivation (Auth)		29	.27*	.18	.08	—.04
3. Low Motivation (Auth)		33	—.06	.12	.15	.15
diff (1, 3)	$t =$		—'	—	—'	—
	$P =$		—	—	—	—
diff (1, 2)	$t =$		—	—	—'	—'
	$P =$		—	—	—	—
diff (2, 3)	$t =$		1.26'	—'	—	—
	$P =$		.10	—	—	—

** $P < .05$
* $P < .10$
' In the predicted direction.

TABLE 20. RELATIONSHIP BETWEEN NONVERBAL REASONING AND RATINGS OF JOB PERFORMANCE FOR HIGH, MODERATE, AND LOW DERIVED MOTIVATION(AUTH) PERSONS

			Pearson r's between Nonverbal Reasoning and:			
		N	Over-all Perform- ance	Summary Appraisal	Over-all Results (a)	Over-all Results (b)
1. High Motivation (Auth)		28	.19	.19	.20	.06
2. Moderate Motivation (Auth)		29	.23	.24*	.07	.15
3. Low Motivation (Auth)		33	.10	.09	—.20	—.25*
diff (1, 3)	$t =$		—′	—′	1.48′	1.18′
	$P =$		—	—	.07	.12
diff (1, 2)	$t =$		—	—	—′	—
	$P =$		—	—	—	—
diff (2, 3)	$t =$		—′	—′	1.00′	1.52′
	$P =$		—	—	.16	.06

* $P < .10$
′ In the predicted direction.

TABLE 21. RELATIONSHIP BETWEEN CLASSIFICATION TEST AND RATINGS OF JOB PERFORMANCE FOR HIGH, MODERATE, AND LOW DERIVED MOTIVATION(AUTH) PERSONS

			Pearson r's between Classification Test and:			
		N	Over-all Perform- ance	Summary Appraisal	Over-all Results (a)	Over-all Results (b)
1. High Motivation (Auth)		28	.08	—.07	—.08	—.10
2. Moderate Motivation (Auth)		29	.05	.03	—.08	.07
3. Low Motivation (Auth)		33	.18	.17	.01	.15
diff (1, 3)	$t =$		—	—	—	—
	$P =$		—	—	—	—
diff (1, 2)	$t =$		—′	—	—	—
	$P =$		—	—	—	—
diff (2, 3)	$t =$		—	—	—	—
	$P =$		—	—	—	—

′ In the predicted direction.

Intelligence and Nonverbal reasoning measures. The Classification Test, on the other hand, shows virtually no differences.

The discrepancy in findings with the two motivation measures requires some comment. One possible explanation hinges around our use of authoritarianism as a component of one of the derived motivation measures. It is possible that other properties of this construct may have opposite effects to those of the motives which it is used to represent. The formula used to obtain derived motivation(Auth) scores is based on the assumption that low authoritarians out-perform high authoritarians. While the evidence obtained in this study [1] indicates that this assumption is generally a valid one, the data suggest that, under low participation conditions, there is a positive correlation between authoritarianism and performance. It is possible that our failure to take this finding into account in calculating our derived motivation(Auth) scores has reduced the validity of the measure.[2]

The present findings support our hypothesis that the effects of ability and motivation on performance are multiplicative as indicated in the formula:

$$\text{Performance} = \text{Ability} \times \text{Motivation}$$

Supporting this model is our finding that ability is more positively related to the performance of highly motivated persons than those with lower motivation. Generally positive correlations between ability and performance were obtained for the high motivation persons and generally negative correlations for low motivation persons. The differences in correlations were more marked between high and low derived motivation(NI) groups than between high and low derived motivation(Auth) persons.

---

[1] See Table 13.

[2] A similar argument can be made for the derived motivation(NI) measure although the findings are not quite as strong.

CHAPTER 5

Discussion and Conclusions

In this chapter we will discuss the findings concerning the joint effects of participation and personality structure and attempt to determine the significance of these findings for theoretical formulations of the relationship between personality and environmental variables. The results and the theoretical and practical implications of the entire study will then be summarized.

5.1. Discussion of Findings

The present study corroborated previous findings that participation in decision-making has positive effects on attitudes and motivation. It was demonstrated further that the magnitude of these effects is a function of certain personality characteristics of the participants. Authoritarians and persons with weak independence needs are apparently unaffected by opportunity to participate in making decisions. On the other hand, equalitarians and those who have strong independence needs develop more positive attitudes toward their job and greater motivation for effective performance through participation.

There is no evidence of any unfavorable effects of participation either on attitudes or on motivation. It should be noted, however, that the sample of supervisors used in this study is not representative of workers in general. It is possible that non-supervisory employees might be more authoritarian and have weaker independence needs which might lead, in the extreme, to negative consequences of participation.

These results suggest the inadequacy of generalizations concerning the effects of participation. Studies which ignore the interaction of participation and personality yield relationships which are nothing more than average effects of participation for all the persons in the group. The statistic used to estimate the degree of relationship underestimates the effects of participation on some persons and overestimates the effects on others.

An adequate theoretical explanation of the effects of participation should include a consideration of the influence of personality variables. In a later section of this chapter we will attempt to explain our findings in terms of more general theories of attitudes and motivation.

A word of caution should be injected here. The findings described hold only for psychological participation. The other three measures included as possible indices of objective participation showed virtually no relationship with one another or with psychological participation. Regardless of the reasons for such lack of agreement, this finding makes it impossible to regard any one or more of these measures as an index of objective participation. Consequently, our conclusions about the interaction of participation and personality must be restricted to psychological participation. The test of the effects of objective participation on persons with different personality characteristics will require the experimental manipulation of this variable or the successful reduction of bias and errors of measurement involved in subjects' reports.

The problem remains of explaining our findings in terms of more general theories of attitudes and motivation. While this study was not explicitly designed to test more general propositions about these variables, an explanation in terms of higher-order processes might provide a useful link with the results from studies of other problems and help point the direction for future research.

We shall use one theoretical framework to explain the effects of participation on attitudes and another to explain the effects on motivation. While it would be ultimately desirable to have a single theory capable of dealing with both attitudes and motivation, there are as yet too many unanswered questions concerning the relationship between these variables to attempt this task here.

5.2. Participation and Attitude

Attitude was defined earlier as "a process which involves affect organized around a conceptual or perceptual nucleus." The amount of affect attached to an object is hypothesized to be a multiplicative function of the strength of motive and the instrumentality of the object for the satisfaction of the motive. Motive is regarded as a relatively stable element of personality and represents a predisposition to obtain satisfaction from a given class of events or consequences. Instrumentality refers to the means–end value of the object for the satisfaction of a motive. There is no necessary relationship between the instrumentality of an object in satisfying different motives. A parent, for example, may be highly instrumental in meeting a child's motive for food but be quite the opposite with respect to motives for affiliation and achievement.

Some of the mathematical properties of this multiplicative model should be noted. Motive or instrumentality scores may take positive or negative values. A negative motive refers to the tendency to experience dissatisfaction from attaining given events or consequences. A person with a strong motive for dependence, for example, might be frustrated by those events which satisfy a motive for independence and might be regarded as having a negative motive for independence. Similarly negative instrumentality refers to the fact that an object hinders rather than facilitates the satisfaction of a motive.

This distinction between positive and negative motives and instrumentalities implies the ability to distinguish a zero point on the underlying variables. Given measures of these two variables and the attitude to which they are related, it is possible to locate this point empirically. The zero point on the motive variable may be determined by relating instrumentality to attitude for various values of motive. Since the effects of motive and instrumentality are multiplicative, a positive value of motive would result in a positive relationship between instrumentality and attitude. A negative value of motive would result in a negative relationship between instrumentality and attitude. Zero motive, representing indifference to the events or consequences, would be that value of motive at which variations in instrumentality have no effect on attitude. Similarly the zero point on instrumentality would be that point at which there is no relationship between motive strength and attitude.

In order to use this theory to explain the findings of this study it is necessary to link amount of participation with the concept of instrumentality of the job. This can be done by making the following assumptions:

1. That participation has terminal or instrumental value for the satisfaction of need for independence and those motives which are characteristic of the equalitarian,
2. That the job will be instrumental to participation.

There is much descriptive evidence for the fact that participation satisfies the needs of the participant. Maier (23), for example, points out that there are a number of different sources of satisfaction involved in the democratic approach to leadership. Participants derive ego satisfaction and pleasure from solving problems, from working in cooperating groups, and from determining their own behavior rather than being forced to do something.

French, *et al.* (10), have also hypothesized that participation satisfies a person's needs to be valued and appreciated. In addition, participation in decision-making is satisfying because it gives participants the opportunity to make decisions which are consistent with their own goals. Thus, workers enjoy participating in making decisions about wages, hours, and working conditions not only because of the social experience, but also because it gives them an opportunity to improve their work situation in these respects.

Although the various sources of satisfaction in participation undoubtedly meet many needs, there is a good basis for assuming that at least some of these sources would be more rewarding to persons who have strong rather than weak independence needs and more rewarding to low than to high authoritarians. It is likely that the need for independence is satisfied by any conditions which permit the individual to determine his own behavior without assistance from or interference by others. A person who participates in making decisions with superiors has greater control over his own actions than one who merely carries out orders. On this basis one would expect participation to satisfy need for independence.

Similarly, participation may be regarded as satisfying a motive for power equality which characterizes equalitarians. Authoritarians are described as preferring strong powerful leaders; equalitarians, on the other hand, prefer more equitable power relationships. Participating in making decisions with superiors may be expected to increase the power equality of the participant and lead to greater satisfaction for equalitarians than for authoritarians.

Throughout the balance of this report we will use the term "motive for power equality" to refer to the motivational aspects of the equalitarian–authoritarian dimension. However, the reader should not lose sight of the fact that other motives might also be associated with this dimension.

The second assumption, namely that the job is seen as instrumental to the satisfaction attained through participation, would seem to be valid where the participation is carried out within the context of the job and is concerned with work-related problems. This condition is clearly met in the present study.

Given these assumptions, an increase in amount of participation would be reflected in an increase in the instrumentality of the job with respect to motives for independence and power equality. According to our theory an attitude toward an object is a multiplicative function of strength of motive and instrumentality. Participation would consequently be expected to have greatest effect on attitudes toward the job where the motives satisfied by participation are strong. This prediction is consistent with the present findings that participation has greatest effect on the attitudes of low authoritarians and persons with high need for independence.

5.3. Participation and Motivation

While the theory discussed so far explains our findings concerning the interaction of participation and personality in the determination of attitudes toward the job, it says nothing about the joint effects of these two variables in determining motivation for effective performance. Most of the aspects of participation cited in connection with the discussion of attitudes involved participation as a source of satisfaction in itself or as a means of satisfying needs through improvements of the job and working conditions. The assumption that participation in decisions satisfies certain motives explains why the job should be seen as instrumental but does not explain, in terms of a tension reduction theory of motivation, why participation should affect the instrumentality of effective performance in that job. In order for participation to affect motivation for effective performance, it would not only have to be a source of satisfaction, but would also have to affect the probability that an individual would be able to attain further satisfaction from performing well in his job. In other words, the participative process would have to involve not only goal attainment but also goal setting.

The theory of motivation [1] to be used here will make a distinction between aroused motivation, which refers to a force acting on the person to behave in a certain direction, and motive, which refers to a predisposition to obtain satisfaction from a given class of events or consequences. A person's aroused motivation to perform a series of acts is hypothesized to be a joint multiplicative function of strength of motive, the value of the incentive offered in the situation, and the expectancy that the acts will lead to the attainment of the incentive. This relationship is expressed in the following formula:

$$\text{Aroused Motivation} = \text{Motive} \times \text{Incentive} \times \text{Expectancy}$$

Incentive and expectancy represent intervening variables which mediate the effects of the situation or environment on behavior. The incentive value of a consequence with respect to a given motive is defined as the extent to which that consequence is expected to satisfy the motive. Expectancy is a cognitive anticipation that performance of some act will be followed by a particular consequence. The strength of expectancy can be represented as the subjective probability of the consequence, given the act.

The multiplicative relationship between these terms and motive in our theory implies that a given situation will be predicted to have different effects on the motivation of individuals with different motive strengths. Similarly, the relationship between strength of motive and performance in a situation will depend on the value of the incentive offered in the situation and the expectancy of attaining it.

Amount of participation may be linked with the incentive

---

[1] This theory is very similar to those previously used by Atkinson (3), Rotter (35), and Tolman (40).

variable in the above theory by making the following assumptions:

1. Persons derive satisfaction from successfully carrying out decisions in which they have participated,
2. The more an individual has influenced a joint decision, the more satisfaction he obtains from its successful execution,
3. The motives for independence and power-equality are satisfied by the successful execution of joint decisions.

These assumptions lead to the conclusion that under high participation conditions the successful execution of decisions would have positive incentive value with respect to the aforementioned motives, and under low participation conditions it would have zero incentive value. Similar assumptions have been made by Maier (23) in his statement that persons become ego-involved in decisions in which they have participated and by French *et al.* (10) in their hypothesis that participation increases the "own forces" on the individual to carry out the decision.

There is an alternative rationale for linking participation to incentive. The following assumptions are similar to those just stated but emphasize negative rather than positive incentives as the basis for the effects of participation on motivation:

1. Persons derive dissatisfaction from successfully executing decisions in which they have had little or no influence,
2. The less influence they have had, the more dissatisfaction they experience from the successful execution of the decision,
3. The motives for independence and power-equality are frustrated by successful execution of decisions in which the individual has had no influence.

These assumptions lead to the conclusion that under low participation conditions the successful execution of decisions would have negative incentive value with respect to the two motives, and under high participation conditions it would have zero incentive value. Similar assumptions are made by French *et al.* (10) in their hypothesis that participation reduces "resistance" forces and by Maier (23) in his hypothesis that participation reduces the amount of frustration of workers.

If amount of participation is linked to incentive value by either or both of the above sets of assumptions, it follows from the motive–incentive–expectancy theory that a person's motivation to perform effectively with respect to a single decision will be a multiplicative function of the strength of his need for independence,[1] the amount of his participation in that decision, and the expectancy that effective performance will lead to successful execution of the decision. Similarly, his motivation for effective performance in his job as a whole will be a multiplicative function of the strength of his need for independence, the extent to which he participates in making decisions in that job, and the average expectancy that effective performance will lead to successful execution of decisions.

The expectancy variable would be a function of such factors as the nature or difficulty of the tasks and the ability of the individual, and be relatively independent of amount of participation. For purposes of the present discussion it will be treated as a constant at some positive value.

It follows from the motive–incentive–expectancy model that the relationship between amount of participation (incentive value) and motivation for effective performance will depend on the strength of those motives that are satisfied by the effective performance. Consequently, this theory may be used to explain our finding that participation increases the motivation for effective performance of persons with strong motives for independence and power equality, but has no effect on those at the opposite ends of these scales.

Our finding that positive correlations between need for independence and performance are found under high participation conditions and generally negative correlations are found under low participation conditions has bearing on the validity of the

---

[1] A similar argument may be made with respect to the authoritarian–equalitarian dimension.

two sets of assumptions just described. Our theory would predict positive correlations between strength of a motive and motivation for effective performance where effective performance was perceived as leading to the satisfaction of that motive (i.e., incentive is positive). On the other hand, negative correlations would be predicted where effective performance was perceived as frustrating the motive (i.e., incentive is negative). Consequently, the findings may be interpreted as meaning that high participation is associated with positive incentives and low participation is associated with negative incentives.

5.4. A Re-examination of the Concept of Participation

In Chapter 3 we raised a question concerning the mechanism(s) at work in the effects of participation on motivation for effective performance. There was some evidence to suggest that the positive correlation between participation and performance was due not only to the positive effects of joint decision-making but also to negative effects of the alternative decision-making processes which are associated with the absence of participation.

In order to get a better idea of what these alternative processes might be and how they might be related to participation let us examine possible mechanisms within a group, consisting of a supervisor and one of his subordinates, for the making of decisions which have future effects on both persons. There are at least three possibilities:

1. The supervisor can make the decision and issue an order to the subordinate,
2. The supervisor can delegate the decision to the subordinate,
3. The supervisor and subordinate can make a joint decision.[1]

---

[1] The amount of participation of a single participant in a joint decision-making situation may range from high positive influence where the participant has affected the decision in the direction of his proposals, to high negative influence where the participant has affected the decision in the direction opposite to his proposals.

Our definition of participation in terms of a joint decision-making process rules out 1 and 2 above. Excluding these two processes from our conceptualization of participation, however, does not aid us in separating them empirically. Both field studies and controlled experiments encounter difficulties in studying the effects of single decision-making processes. Since the number of areas in which decisions have to be made by organizations is fairly constant, an increase in the number of jointly made decisions invariably results in a decrease in the number of decisions made by one or both of the alternative methods. Similarly, an increase in the number of decisions made unilaterally by the supervisor (#1) or delegated to the subordinate (#2) may be expected to decrease the number of joint decisions.

The fact that a variable is difficult to separate from other variables does not necessarily detract from its value in explaining behavior. However, there is always the possibility that findings attributed to one variable may be due to the effects of others with which it is linked. In the present study, for example, there is some evidence to suggest that at least some of the effects attributed to participation are due to domination which is associated with low participation. Whenever possible, all variables that are linked in this manner should be measured in an attempt to determine more accurately the source of observed effects.

For example, low participation in decision-making may be due to more or less complete autonomy on the part of the individual or to more or less complete domination of that individual by his superior. Since autonomy and domination probably have very different psychological effects, it becomes extremely important to measure these decision-making processes independently of amount of participation.

The problems associated with participation and its relationships with other decision-making processes might be solved by an alternative conceptualization of participation as amount of influence in decision-making, regardless of whether the decisions were made in a joint or individual manner. A person who had complete freedom in making a decision might be regarded as having 100 per cent influence in that decision, while a person who was ordered to carry out a decision made by his superior might be regarded as having no influence.

Although this different conception of participation eliminates the necessity of separating various decision-making processes, its ultimate value will depend on the relative importance of inter-personal aspects of the decision-making processes as compared with the amount of influence that they afford the individual. To the extent that complete autonomy in the making of decisions has similar effects to high influence in joint decision-making and domination has similar effects to low influence in joint decision-making, the new conceptualization will add clarity. The answer to this problem must rest with future research.

The profusion of already existing definitions of participation suggests that a new term be used to refer to the alternative conception. For purposes of this paper we will use the term "self-determination" to refer to the amount of an individual's influence in decisions which have future effects on him, regardless of the nature of the process by which these decisions are made. We will continue to use the term "participation" to refer to amount of influence in joint decision-making.

5.5. Summary and Implications

The findings in this study have been interpreted as supporting our hypothesis that the effects of participation in decision-making depend on certain personality characteristics of the participant. The evidence suggests that authoritarianism and need for independence interact with participation in determining attitudes toward the job and motivation for effective performance.

As we have pointed out, it has been necessary to restrict our conclusions to psychological participation. No measure of objective participation has been obtained, and extension of our findings to include its effects will require further research.

An attempt was made to interpret the present findings in terms of more general theories of attitudes and motivation. The hypothesis that a person's attitude toward an object is a multiplicative function of strength of motive and the instrumentality of the object to the satisfaction of that motive was found to be useful in explaining our findings concerning the joint effects of participation and personality on attitudes toward the job. If participation in decision-making satisfies certain motives and if the job is perceived as instrumental to that participation, then it follows that participation would be related to the instrumentality of the job with respect to these motives. Consequently the motive–instrumentality hypothesis would predict that the effects of participation on attitudes toward the job would be directly proportional to the strength of the motives satisfied by the participation.

The hypothesis that a person's aroused motivation to perform a series of acts is a multiplicative function of strength of motive, the value of the incentive offered in the situation, and the expectancy that the acts will lead to the attainment of the incentive, was able to explain the findings concerning the joint effects of participation and personality on motivation for effective performance. If it is assumed that the relative amount of satisfaction that a person gets from successfully executing the decision is a function of the amount of his participation in these decisions, participation may be linked with the incentive value of successful execution of decisions. According to the motive–incentive–expectancy theory the effects of participation on aroused motivation may consequently be expected to vary with the strength of those motives satisfied by successful execution of the joint decisions.

Some evidence was obtained in this study to suggest that the positive relationship between participation and both attitudes and motivation is due, at least in part, to the negative effects of alternative decision-making processes which are associated with the absence of participation. The concept of self-determination, defined as the amount of influence that an individual has on decisions which have future effects on him, was offered as a possible solution to the numerous problems involved in isolating the effects of joint decision-making processes. Further research is needed to determine the value of this concept.

The findings in the second aspect of the study on the joint effects of ability and motivation suggest that ability is more positively related to the performance of highly motivated workers than of those with lower motivation. While different results may be obtained for different tasks, the present findings suggest that the effects of ability and motivation are multiplicative rather than additive. This relationship may be summarized in the following formula:

$$\text{Performance} = \text{Ability} \times \text{Motivation}$$

The theoretical implications of the present study are evident from our previous discussion of the assumptions and postulates needed to account for our findings. The study also points the direction for future research, which, if confirming our results, could have significant social consequences.

The immediate need is for a corroboration of the present findings using suitable experimental controls and objective measures of performance. The logic underlying the present design could be used then to study the effects of other environmental variables such as leadership practices, group norms, etc., on persons with different personality characteristics.

This line of research might have the effect of broadening the field of personnel selection from an exclusive focus on aptitudes and abilities to a consideration of the potential motivation of applicants. This process would require the measurement of the strength of motives and other personality characteristics as well as the measurement of relevant properties of the work situation (type of job, supervision, etc.). Our present findings indicate these two sets of variables may be used simultaneously to yield a prediction of motivation for effective performance. This measure would in turn be combined with measures of ability to yield a final prediction of the applicant's job performance.

A second possible practical implication of research of the type reported here would be the modification of leadership training courses to take into consideration the fact that there is no one correct method of supervision. Practices or methods which are appropriate for dealing with persons with one set of personality characteristics may be entirely inappropriate for others. Similarly, different methods of training and changing attitudes may be effective with persons with different personalities. Some evidence on this problem has been obtained by McClintock (28).

Finally, our evidence concerning the joint effects of ability and motivation suggests that management efforts to obtain and develop individuals with skill and ability and to motivate these individuals must proceed concurrently. The benefits accruing from selection and training programs depend upon the organization's previous success in creating conditions conducive to high motivation. Similarly, the value of human relations training and other procedures designed to have the ultimate effect of motivating individuals will depend on the level of these individuals' aptitude and ability.

THE MEASURES

Need for Independence *

†1. How important is it for you to feel that you can run your life without depending upon people who are older and more experienced than you? (Check one)
1 Not at all
2 Slightly
3 Somewhat
4 Very
5 Extremely

†2. How often do you find that you can carry out other people's suggestions without changing them any? (Check one)
5 Rarely
4 Sometimes
3 Often
2 Very often
1 Almost always

†3. How much humility do you think you should show to those whom you respect and admire? (Check one)
5 None at all

4 A little
3 Some
2 Quite a bit
1 Very much

†4. How much respect do you think should be shown to a judge even outside his courtroom? (Check one)
5 None at all
4 Some
3 Quite a bit
2 Very much
1 Extremely much

†5. How much do you usually want the person who is in charge of a group you are in to tell you what to do? (Check one)
5 Not at all
4 A little
3 Somewhat
2 Quite a bit
1 Very much

6. When you have a problem how much do you like to think it

---

* Most of the items making up this measure were taken from a questionnaire developed and used by Tannenbaum and Allport (39).

† Also included in the short form.

through yourself without help from others? (Check one)

    1 Not at all
    2 Somewhat
    3 Quite a bit
    4 Very much
    5 Extremely much

7. How much respect do you think people should show to policemen? (Check one)

    5 None at all
    4 Some
    3 Quite a bit
    2 Very much
    1 Extremely much

*8. How hard do you find it to disagree with others even in your own thinking? (Check one)

    5 Not at all
    4 Slightly
    3 Somewhat
    2 Quite
    1 Very

9. How much do you think that the leaders of organizations to which you belong have the right to expect certain things from you to which you should conform? (Check one)

    5 Not at all
    4 A little
    3 Somewhat
    2 Quite a bit
    1 Very much

10. How much do you feel that you are not as good in most things as people who are older and more experienced than you? (Check one)

    5 Not at all
    4 A little

    3 Somewhat
    2 Quite a bit
    1 Very much

11. In school how much did you dislike teachers who had forceful and dominant personalities? (Check one)

    1 Not at all
    2 A little
    3 Somewhat
    4 Quite a bit
    5 Very much

*12. If you have thought about something and come to a conclusion, how hard is it for someone else to change your mind? (Check one)

    1 Not at all
    2 Somewhat
    3 Quite
    4 Very
    5 Extremely

13. How much do you feel that officers of the law should tell people what to do rather than ask them? (Check one)

    5 Not at all
    4 A little
    3 Somewhat
    2 Quite a bit
    1 Very much

14. If you were to go to night school under which of these conditions would you learn best? (Check one)

    5 If I were left completely alone to seek out whatever I wanted
    4 If I were given suggestions from teachers as to what might be the best to study

---

* Also included in the short form.

3 If I were given some suggestions and some assignments to complete

2 If I were instructed, given assignments, and tested occasionally

1 If I were given daily instructions, daily assignments and frequent tests

*15. How much do you dislike being told to do something by a superior that is contrary to your wishes? (Check one)

1 Not at all
2 A little
3 Somewhat
4 Quite a bit
5 Very much

16. How often do you base your actions on your own judgments and evaluations? (Check one)

5 Almost always
4 Very often
3 Often
2 Sometimes
1 Rarely

Attitude Toward Job

1. How well do you like supervisory work? (Check one)

5 I like it very much
4 I like it pretty well
3 I like it in some ways, but not in others
2 I don't like it very much
1 I don't like it at all

2. How much chance does your job give you to do the things you are best at? (Check one)

5 A very good chance to do the things I am best at
4 A fairly good chance
3 Some chance
2 Very little chance
1 No chance to do the things I am best at

3. How good is your immediate superior in dealing with people? (Check one)

5 He does an excellent job in dealing with people
4 A very good job
3 A fairly good job
2 A fairly poor job
1 A poor job in dealing with people

Psychological Participation

1. In general, how much say or influence do you feel you have on what goes on in your station? (Check one)

5 A very great deal of influence
4 A great deal of influence
3 Quite a bit of influence
2 Some influence
1 Little or no influence

2. Do you feel you can influence the decisions of your immediate superior regarding things about which you are concerned? (Check one)

5 I can influence him to a very great extent
4 To a considerable extent
3 To some extent
2 To a very little extent
1 I can not influence him at all

---

* Also included in the short form.

3. Does your immediate superior ask your opinion when a problem comes up that involves your work? (Check one)

   5 He always asks my opinion
   4 Often asks
   3 Sometimes asks
   2 Seldom asks
   1 He never asks my opinion

4. If you have a suggestion for improving the job or changing the setup in some way, how easy is it for you to get your ideas across to your immediate superior? (Check one)

   1 It is very difficult to get my ideas across
   2 Somewhat difficult
   3 Not too easy
   4 Fairly easy
   5 It is very easy to get my ideas across

Authoritarianism Measure *

The following questions are not directed towards your work or the things you do at _____ but rather towards your life as a whole, both past and present. In answering these questions we are interested in what you as a person believe and feel in all your activities.

1. Obedience and respect for authority are the most important virtues children should learn. (Check one)

   5 Strongly agree
   4 Agree
   3 I can't make up my mind
   2 Disagree
   1 Strongly disagree

2. A person who has bad manners, habits, and breeding can hardly expect to get along with decent people. (Check one)

   5 Strongly agree
   4 Agree
   3 I can't make up my mind
   2 Disagree
   1 Strongly disagree

3. If people would talk less and work more, everybody would be better off. (Check one)

   5 Strongly agree
   4 Agree
   3 I can't make up my mind
   2 Disagree
   1 Strongly disagree

4. Science has its place, but there are many important things that can never possibly be understood by the human mind. (Check one)

   5 Strongly agree
   4 Agree
   3 I can't make up my mind
   2 Disagree
   1 Strongly disagree

5. Every person should have complete faith in some supernatural power whose decisions he obeys without question. (Check one)

   5 Strongly agree
   4 Agree
   3 I can't make up my mind
   2 Disagree
   1 Strongly disagree

---

* The following items were taken from Forms 40 and 45 of the *F* scale developed by Adorno, et al. (1).

6. Young people sometimes get re-
bellious ideas, but as they grow
up they ought to get over them
and settle down. (Check one)
   5 Strongly agree
   4 Agree
   3 I can't make up my mind
   2 Disagree
   1 Strongly disagree

7. What this country needs most,
more than laws and political
programs, is a few courageous,
tireless, devoted leaders in whom
the people can put their faith.
(Check one)
   5 Strongly agree
   4 Agree
   3 I can't make up my mind
   2 Disagree
   1 Strongly disagree

8. No sane, normal, decent person
could ever think of hurting a
close friend or relative. (Check
one)
   5 Strongly agree
   4 Agree
   3 I can't make up my mind
   2 Disagree
   1 Strongly disagree

9. What the youth needs most is
strict discipline, rugged determination, and the will to work
and fight for family and country.
(Check one)
   5 Strongly agree
   4 Agree
   3 I can't make up my mind
   2 Disagree
   1 Strongly disagree

10. An insult to our honor should always be punished. (Check one)
   5 Strongly agree

4 Agree
3 I can't make up my mind
2 Disagree
1 Strongly disagree

11. Sex crimes, such as rape and at-
tacks on children, deserve more
than mere imprisonment; such
criminals ought to be publicly
whipped, or worse. (Check one)
   5 Strongly agree
   4 Agree
   3 I can't make up my mind
   2 Disagree
   1 Strongly disagree

12. There is hardly anything lower
than a person who does not feel
a great love, gratitude, and respect for his parents. (Check
one)
   5 Strongly agree
   4 Agree
   3 I can't make up my mind
   2 Disagree
   1 Strongly disagree

13. Most of our social problems
would be solved if we could
somehow get rid of the immoral,
crooked, and feeble-minded people. (Check one)
   5 Strongly agree
   4 Agree
   3 I can't make up my mind
   2 Disagree
   1 Strongly disagree

14. Homosexuals are hardly better
than criminals and ought to be
severely punished. (Check one)
   5 Strongly agree
   4 Agree
   3 I can't make up my mind
   2 Disagree
   1 Strongly disagree

15 When a person has a problem or worry, it is best for him not to think about it, but to keep busy with more cheerful things. (Check one)
  5 Strongly agree
  4 Agree
  3 I can't make up my mind
  2 Disagree
  1 Strongly disagree

16. Nowadays more and more people are prying into matters that should remain personal and private. (Check one)
  5 Strongly agree
  4 Agree
  3 I can't make up my mind
  2 Disagree
  1 Strongly disagree

17. Some people are born with an urge to jump from high places. (Check one)
  5 Strongly agree
  4 Agree
  3 I can't make up my mind
  2 Disagree
  1 Strongly disagree

18. People can be divided into two distinct classes: the weak and the strong. (Check one)
  5 Strongly agree
  4 Agree
  3 I can't make up my mind
  2 Disagree
  1 Strongly disagree

19. Some day it will probably be shown that astrology can explain a lot of things. (Check one)
  5 Strongly agree
  4 Agree
  3 I can't make up my mind
  2 Disagree
  1 Strongly disagree

20. No weaknesses or difficulty can hold us back if we have enough will power. (Check one)
  5 Strongly agree
  4 Agree
  3 I can't make up my mind
  2 Disagree
  1 Strongly disagree

21. Most people don't realize how much our lives are controlled by plots hatched in secret places. (Check one)
  5 Strongly agree
  4 Agree
  3 I can't make up my mind
  2 Disagree
  1 Strongly disagree

22. Human nature being what it is, there will always be war and conflict. (Check one)
  5 Strongly agree
  4 Agree
  3 I can't make up my mind
  2 Disagree
  1 Strongly disagree

23. Familiarity breeds contempt. (Check one)
  5 Strongly agree
  4 Agree
  3 I can't make up my mind
  2 Disagree
  1 Strongly disagree

24. Nowadays when so many different kinds of people move around and mix together so much, a person has to protect himself especially carefully against catching an infection or disease from them. (Check one)
  5 Strongly agree
  4 Agree
  3 I can't make up my mind
  2 Disagree
  1 Strongly disagree

25. The wild sex life of the old Greeks and Romans was tame compared to some of the goings-on in this country, even in places where people might least expect it. (Check one)

   5 Strongly agree

   4 Agree

   3 I can't make up my mind

   2 Disagree

   1 Strongly disagree

APPENDIX II

TABLE 22. VARIANCE ESTIMATES AND F-RATIOS FOR PERSONS WITH DIFFERENT
PERSONALITY CHARACTERISTICS ON INDEPENDENT AND
DEPENDENT VARIABLES

	Psychological Participation		Attitude Toward the Job		Over-all Performance		Summary Appraisal	
	s^2	N	s^2	N	s^2	N	s^2	N
1. High Need Independence	4.51	38	3.81	38	16.03	33	7.88	33
2. Moderate Need Independence	3.64	32	2.16	32	13.44	28	8.44	28
3. Low Need Independence	3.86	38	2.38	38	13.35	35	6.29	35
$F_{(1, 3)}$	1.17		1.60		1.20		1.25	
$F_{(1, 2)}$	1.24		1.76**		1.19		1.07	
$F_{(2, 3)}$	1.06		1.10		1.01		1.34	
4. High Authoritarianism	3.70	34	2.06	34	15.96	30	8.31	30
5. Moderate Authoritarianism	2.70	34	3.09	34	12.25	33	5.75	33
6. Low Authoritarianism	4.76	39	3.24	39	13.26	32	7.81	32
$F_{(4, 6)}$	1.29		1.57		1.20		1.06	
$F_{(4, 5)}$	1.37		1.50		1.30		1.44	
$F_{(5, 6)}$	1.76**		1.05		1.08		1.36	

** $P < .05$

APPENDIX III

TABLE 23. MEAN SCORES ON ATTITUDE TOWARD THE JOB FOR PERSONS WITH DIFFERENT PERSONALITY CHARACTERISTICS UNDER HIGH, MODERATE, AND LOW PSYCHOLOGICAL PARTICIPATION CONDITIONS

	High Participation		Moderate Participation		Low Participation	
	N	Mean	N	Mean	N	Mean
Total Group	31	13.39[a]	39	12.51	38	12.18
High Need Independence	10	14.00	14	12.07	14	11.86
Moderate Need Independence	9	13.67	11	12.27	12	12.25
Low Need Independence	12	12.67	14	13.14	12	12.50
High Authoritarian	7	12.71	11	12.73	16	12.38
Moderate Authoritarian	11	13.73	14	12.36	9	12.56
Low Authoritarian	12	13.42	14	12.86	13	11.69

[a] Theoretical range for attitude toward the job is 3–15.

TABLE 24. MEAN SCORES ON ATTITUDE TOWARD THE JOB FOR COMBINATIONS OF NEED FOR INDEPENDENCE AND AUTHORITARIANISM UNDER HIGH, MODERATE, AND LOW PSYCHOLOGICAL PARTICIPATION CONDITIONS

	High Participation		Moderate Participation		Low Participation	
	$\overline{X}$	N	$\overline{X}$	N	$\overline{X}$	N
High Need Independence & Low Authoritarian	14.22	9	12.67	9	11.45	11
High Need Independence & High Authoritarian	13.71	7	11.00	9	12.30	10
Low Need Independence & Low Authoritarian	12.75	8	13.08	12	12.50	6
Low Need Independence & High Authoritarian	12.50	6	13.11	9	12.64	11

83

TABLE 25. MEAN SCORES ON OVER-ALL PERFORMANCE FOR PERSONS WITH DIFFERENT
PERSONALITY CHARACTERISTICS UNDER HIGH, MODERATE, AND LOW
PSYCHOLOGICAL PARTICIPATION CONDITIONS

	High Participation		Moderate Participation		Low Participation	
	$\overline{X}$	N	$\overline{X}$	N	$\overline{X}$	N
Total group	12.19[a]	31	11.15	34	10.58	31
High Need Independence	12.70	10	11.08	13	9.80	10
Moderate Need Independence	13.56	9	10.88	8	11.45	11
Low Need Independence	10.75	12	11.38	13	10.40	10
High Authoritarian	10.29	7	9.82	11	11.08	12
Moderate Authoritarian	14.45	11	12.38	13	12.67	9
Low Authoritarian	12.92	12	13.00	10	10.50	10
High Need Independence & Low Authoritarian	13.67	9	13.38	8	11.22	9
High Need Independence & High Authoritarian	12.14	7	9.33	9	9.88	8
Low Need Independence & Low Authoritarian	11.50	8	10.78	9	10.20	5
Low Need Independence & High Authoritarian	10.17	6	11.38	8	10.78	9

[a] Theoretical range for over-all performance is 1–20.

TABLE 26. MEAN SCORES ON SUMMARY APPRAISAL FOR PERSONS WITH DIFFERENT
PERSONALITY CHARACTERISTICS UNDER HIGH, MODERATE, AND LOW
PSYCHOLOGICAL PARTICIPATION CONDITIONS

	High Participation		Moderate Participation		Low Participation	
	$\overline{X}$	N	$\overline{X}$	N	$\overline{X}$	N
Total group	13.58[a]	31	12.41	34	12.39	31
High Need Independence	13.60	10	12.31	13	12.10	10
Moderate Need Independence	14.56	9	12.13	8	11.91	11
Low Need Independence	12.83	12	12.69	13	13.20	10
High Authoritarian	12.57	7	11.64	11	13.00	16
Moderate Authoritarian	12.18	11	10.85	13	10.00	9
Low Authoritarian	13.08	12	13.30	10	11.40	10
High Need Independence & Low Authoritarian	13.67	9	13.88	8	11.67	9
High Need Independence & High Authoritarian	13.86	7	11.22	9	12.63	8
Low Need Independence & Low Authoritarian	12.75	8	12.33	9	12.00	5
Low Need Independence & High Authoritarian	13.67	6	12.38	8	13.11	9

[a] Theoretical range for summary appraisal is 1–20.

TABLE 27. RELATIONSHIP BETWEEN PEER-REPORTED PARTICIPATION AND BOTH ATTITUDE
TOWARD THE JOB AND JOB PERFORMANCE FOR PERSONS WITH
DIFFERENT PERSONALITY CHARACTERISTICS

	Pearson r's between peer-reported participation and:							
	Attitude Toward the Job		Drive		Over-all Perform-ance		Summary Appraisal	
	r	N	r	N	r	N	r	N
Total Group	.19**	102	.21**	96	.33***	96	.31***	96
1. High Need Independence	.44***	33	.33**	29	.31**	29	.41**	29
2. Moderate Need Independence	.12	31	.26	22	.53***	28	.50***	28
3. Low Need Independence	.11	38	.13	35	.13	35	.14	35
diff (1, 3) $t =$	1.44′		—′		1.19′		1.15′	
$P =$	.07		—		.12		.12	
diff (1, 2) $t =$	1.35′		—′		—		—	
$P =$	.09		—		—		—	
diff (2, 3) $t =$	—′		—′		1.70′		1.52′	
$P =$	—		—		.04		.06	
4. High Authoritarian	.13	31	.19	29	.42**	29	.52***	29
5. Moderate Authoritarian	.20	34	.05	33	.24*	33	.14	33
6. Low Authoritarian	.15	36	.30*	29	.18	29	.21	29
diff (4, 6) $t =$	—′		—′		—		1.32	
$P =$	—		—		—		.18	
diff (4, 5) $t =$	—′		—		—		1.63	
$P =$	—		—		—		.10	
diff (5, 6) $t =$	—		—′		—		—′	
$P =$	—		—		—		—	

*** $P < .01$
** $P < .05$
* $P < .10$
′ In the predicted direction.

TABLE 28. RELATIONSHIP BETWEEN SUPERIOR-REPORTED PARTICIPATION AND BOTH
ATTITUDE TOWARD THE JOB AND JOB PERFORMANCE FOR PERSONS
WITH DIFFERENT PERSONALITY CHARACTERISTICS

	Pearson r's between superior-reported participation and:							
	Attitude Toward the Job		Drive		Over-all Perform- ance		Summary Appraisal	
	r	N	r	N	r	N	r	N
Total group	.20*	61	.11	50	.23*	50	.22*	50
1. High Need Independence	.32*	19	.33	14	.39*	14	.29	14
2. Moderate Need Independence	.11	16	.05	13	.33	13	.10	13
3. Low Need Independence	.12	26	—.03	23	.31	23	.14	23
diff (1, 3) $t =$	—′		—′		—′		—′	
$P =$	—		—		--		—	
diff (1, 2) $t =$	—′		—′		—′		—′	
$P =$	—		—		—		—	
diff (2, 3) $t =$	—		—′		—′		—	
$P =$	—		—		—		—	
4. High Authoritarian	.23	26	.20	22	.07	22	.06	22
5. Moderate Authoritarian	.10	17	.06	16	.59**	16	.42*	16
6. Low Authoritarian	.30	18	—.16	22	.08	22	.16	22
diff (4, 6) $t =$	—′		1.12		—′		—′	
$P =$	—		—		—		—	
diff (4, 5) $t =$	—		—		1.69′		1.08′	
$P =$	—		—		.05		.14	
diff (5, 6) $t =$	—′		—		1.67		—	
$P =$	—		—		.10		—	

** $P < .05$
* $P < .10$
′ In the predicted direction.

TABLE 29. RELATIONSHIP BETWEEN SUBORDINATE-REPORTED PARTICIPATION AND BOTH ATTITUDE TOWARD THE JOB AND JOB PERFORMANCE FOR PERSONS WITH DIFFERENT PERSONALITY CHARACTERISTICS

	Pearson r's between subordinate-reported participation and:							
	Attitude Toward the Job		Drive		Over-all Perform-ance		Summary Appraisal	
	r	N	r	N	r	N	r	N
Total group	.16**	101	.15*	96	.20**	96	.20**	96
1. High Need Independence	.21	35	.26*	30	.17	30	.08	30
2. Moderate Need Independence	.06	29	—.06	27	—.33*	27	—.08	27
3. Low Need Independence	.19	37	—.15	34	.01	34	.17	34
diff (1, 3) $t=$	—'		1.62'		—'		—	
$P=$	—		.05		—		—	
diff (1, 2) $t=$	—'		1.18'		1.82'		—'	
$P=$	—		.12		.03		—	
diff (2, 3) $t=$	—		—'		1.30		—	
$P=$	—		—		—		—	
4. High Authoritarian	.02	29	.01	27	.10	27	.36**	27
5. Moderate Authoritarian	.38**	34	.15	33	.02	33	—.04	33
6. Low Authoritarian	.10	37	—.07	30	.00	30	.01	30
diff (4, 6) $t=$	—'		—		—		1.32	
$P=$	—		—		—		—	
diff (4, 5) $t=$	1.41'		—'		—		1.56	
$P=$	.08		—		—		.12	
diff (5, 6) $t=$	1.20		—		—		—'	
$P=$	—		—		—		—	

** $P < .05$
* $P < .10$
' In the predicted direction.

BIBLIOGRAPHY

1. Adorno, T., Frenkel-Brunswik, E., Levinson, D. J., and Sanford, R. N., *The Authoritarian Personality*. New York: Harper, 1950.

2. Allport, G. W., "The historical background of modern social psychology," In *Handbook of Social Psychology*, ed. G. Lindzey. Cambridge: Addison-Wesley, 1954, pp. 3–56.

3. Atkinson, J. W., "Motivational determinants of risk-taking behavior," *Psychol. Rev.*, 1957, **64**, 359–372.

4. Atkinson, J. W., and Reitman, W. R., "Performance as a function of motive strength and expectancy of goal attainment," *J. Abnorm. Soc. Psychol.*, 1956, **53**, 361–366.

5. Baumgartel, H., "Leadership, motivations, and attitudes in research laboratories," *J. Soc. Issues*, 1956, **12**, 24–31.

6. Bennett, E. B., "Discussion, decision, commitment and consensus in 'group decision'," *Hum. Relat.*, 1955, **8**, 251–273.

7. Coch, L., and French, J. R. P., Jr., "Overcoming resistance to change," *Hum. Relat.*, 1948, **1**, 512–532.

8. Cronbach, L. J., "The two disciplines of scientific psychology," *Amer. Psychologist*, 1957, **12**, 671–684.

9. French, E. G., "Effects of interaction of achievement, motivation, and intelligence on problem solving success," *Amer. Psychologist*, 1957, **12**, 399–400. (Abstract)

10. French, J. R. P., Jr., Israel, J., and Ås, D., "An experiment on participation in a Norwegian factory," *Hum. Relat.*, 1960, **13**, in press.

11. Freud, S., *Group Psychology and the Analysis of the Ego*. London: International Psychoanalytic Press, 1922.

12. Gibb, C. A., "Leadership" in *Handbook of Social Psychology*, ed. G. Lindzey. Cambridge: Addison-Wesley, 1954, pp. 877–920.

13. Jacobson, E., "Foreman-steward participation practices and worker

attitudes in a unionized factory," Unpublished doctoral dissertation, University of Michigan, 1951.

14. Katz, D., "Special review. Handbook of social psychology." *Psychol. Bull.,* 1955, **52,** 346–353.

15. Krech, D., and Crutchfield, R. S., *Theory and Problems of Social Psychology.* New York: McGraw-Hill, 1948.

16. Lawrence, L. C., and Smith, P. C., "Group decision and employee participation," *J. Appl. Psychol.,* 1955, **39,** 334–337.

17. Levine, J., and Butler, J., "Lecture versus group discussion in changing behavior," *J. Appl. Psychol.,* 1952, **36,** 29–33.

18. Lewin, K., "Group decision and social change," in *Readings in Social Psychology,* eds. T. M. Newcomb & E. L. Hartley. New York: Henry Holt, 1947, pp. 330–344.

19. Lewin, K., "Frontiers in group dynamics," in *Field Theory in Social Science,* ed. D. Cartwright. New York: Harper, 1951, pp. 188–237.

20. Lewin, K., Lippitt, R., and White, R., "Patterns of aggressive behavior in experimentally created social climates," *J. Soc. Psychol.,* 1939, **10,** 271–299.

21. Likert, R., "Effective supervision: An adaptive and relative process." *Personnel Psychol.,* 1958, **11,** 317–332.

22. Maier, N. R. F., "The quality of group decisions as influenced by the discussion leader," *Hum. Relat.,* 1950, **3,** 155–174.

23. Maier, N. R. F., *Principles of Human Relations.* New York: Wiley, 1952.

24. Maier, N. R. F., "An experimental test of the effect of training on discussion leadership," *Hum. Relat.,* 1953, **6,** 161–173.

25. Maier, N. R. F., *Psychology in Industry.* (2nd ed.) Boston: Houghton Mifflin, 1955.

26. Mann, F. C., and Baumgartel, H., *Absences and Employee Attitudes in an Electric Power Company.* Ann Arbor: Survey Research Center, 1952.

27. Mann, F. C., and Baumgartel, H., "The supervisor's views on costs." New York: American Management Association; Office Management Series No. 138, 1954, 3–21.

28. McClintock, C. G., "Personality factors in attitude change." Unpublished doctoral dissertation, University of Michigan, 1957.

29. McGregor, D., "Getting effective leadership in an industrial organization," *Advanc. Management,* 1944, **9,** 148–153.

30. Morse, N. C., and Reimer, E., "The experimental change of a major organizational variable," *J. Abnorm. Soc. Psychol.,* 1956, **52,** 120–129.

31. Murray, H. A., *Explorations in Personality.* New York: Oxford University Press, 1938.

32. Peak, H., "Attitude and motivation," in *Nebraska Symposium on Motivation.* Lincoln: University of Nebraska Press, 1955, pp. 149–188.

33. Radke, M., and Klisurich, D., "Experiments in changing food habits," *J. Amer. Diet. Assn.,* 1947, **23,** 403–409.

34. Ross, I., and Zander, A., "Need satisfactions and employee turnover," *Personnel Psychol.,* 1957, **10,** 327–338.

35. Rotter, J. B., *Social Learning and Clinical Psychology.* New York: Prentice-Hall, 1954.

36. Sanford, F. H., *Authoritarianism and Leadership.* Philadelphia: Institute for Research in Human Relations, 1950.

37. Simmons, W., "The group approach to weight reduction. I: A review of the project," *J. Amer. Diet. Assn.,* 1954, **30,** 437–441.

38. Tannenbaum, A., "The relationship between personality and group structure." Unpublished doctoral dissertation, Syracuse University, 1954.

39. Tannenbaum, A., and Allport, F. H., "Personality structure and group structure: an interpretative study of their relationship through an event-structure hypothesis," *J. Abnorm. Soc. Psychol.,* 1956, **53,** 272–280.

40. Tolman, E. C., "Principles of performance," *Psychol. Rev.,* 1955, **62,** 315–326.

41. Wickert, R., "Turnover and employee's feelings of ego-involvement in the day-to-day operation of a company," *Personnel Psychol.,* 1951, **4,** 185–197.